9 to 5
and
Spiritually Alive

9 to 5
and
Spiritually Alive

Pour Yourself a Fresh
Cup of Life

SHEILA JONES

DPI
DISCIPLESHIP
PUBLICATIONS
INTERNATIONAL

Boston

---

9 to 5 and Spiritually Alive
©1997 by Discipleship Publications International
One Merrill Street, Woburn, MA 01801
www.dpibooks.com

Printed in the United States of America
Cover and interior design:Chris Costello

ISBN 1-57782-035-5

To my husband, Tom,
whose courage, compassion and conviction
always call me higher.
I love you with all my heart.

CONTENTS

Acknowledgments

My deepest thanks to the many busy working women who have taken the time to respond to my survey, individual questions and interviews in order to contribute to the authenticity and relevance of this book. I could not have done it without your help. You are indeed the backbone of *9 to 5 and Spiritually Alive!*

Thanks also to Tom Jones, Kim Hanson and Lisa Morris for their editorial midwifery; their input and support were invaluable in the birth of this book.

INTRODUCTION

⟡

9 to 5

Spiritually Alive

One bleary brown eye reluctantly opened and joined the other. *Surely it is not time to get up!* 6:00 a.m. The six and two zeros did their hazy morning dance. She slapped the snooze button, hoping she could squeeze an hour or two out of the next ten minutes. But, as usual, ten minutes later in typical Swiss precision, the alarm blared again.

"Up! Up! Get up!" her mind said.

"Down! Down! Stay down!" her body pled.

Her mind won. Her body dutifully followed. Another work day...have quiet time, find clean clothes, iron out wrinkles, eat quick breakfast. She crawls. Time flies.

Sometimes Marsha wished she could get a better handle on her mornings. She wished she could get a better handle on her whole day, especially on her job. She felt so many pressures and demands. And sometimes she felt very alone because of the convictions she held as a disciple. *How can I work 9 to 5 and stay spiritually alive?*

Throwing her jacket over her shoulder, she took a deep breath and resolved that tomorrow she would work on finding some answers to the questions that floated around in her heart and mind. She shut the front door behind her and faced another challenging day.

∽

"Workin' 9 to 5 / What a way to make a livin'," sings Dolly Parton. Whether it is *9 to 5* or *8 to 3* or *10 to 6*, working does seem to be the *only* way to make a living. But as women who are followers of Jesus Christ, how can we be "spiritually alive" no matter what hours we work? That is the challenge and the goal. We must be focused and responsible on our jobs, but never allow our jobs to distract us from our real purpose in life: becoming like Jesus.

For several years I led a group of working women who were disciples. We called ourselves "9 to 5 and Spiritually Alive." We spent time together getting our own moorings in a morally drifting work world. We reached out to our workmates, bringing them to brunches and Bible studies that were relevant to their needs as working women. Our desire was to be faithful to Jesus as we worked to help support our families—a challenging task indeed. But being faithful to Jesus is challenging whether we work outside the home or inside the home. No matter what we do, the goal requires all we are and have.

Spiritually Alive or Barely Alive?

After we started the 9-to-5 group, my daughter bought me a huge yellow button with large red letters that read: "9 to 5 and barely alive!" Maybe that's how you feel at times on the job—*barely alive*, physically and spiritually. This book was written to be a practical encouragement to you.

All the current literature for women tells us that Superwoman and Supermom are dead. Certainly, I am glad to hear of their demise. The only problem is, whoever is left still has a lot to do! And that *whoever* is you and I, working women.

More and more women are entering the workforce. The US Department of Labor Women's Bureau says that by the year 2000, 85 percent of women between 19 and 54 will be employed, thus making up the majority of the workforce. That's a lot of working women! I am part of a church of more than 4000 members, of which more than half are women. After doing an informal survey several years ago, I found that around 75 percent of the adult women (single and married) work outside the home. I also found that 66 percent of the married women work outside the home. In addition, 36 percent of all the working women are working mothers (single and married). You may have difficulty corralling all these numbers, but basically they tell us that a lot of women in the church are daily in work settings and need help and encouragement to remain spiritually alive.

Who Is This Book For?

This book was written for all the *Marshas* in the workforce, married and single. It was written to help us be "overcomers," not just "copers." We deal with the stress caused by structured work hours, long commutes and pressing responsibilities at home and in the ministry. We also experience pressures on the job itself: a workmate who is hard to get along with, a manager who cannot manage to manage, a boss who blows up at us when he is under the gun from "upstairs," and the temptation to get involved in gossip, back-stabbing, jealousy, flirting and misuse of time.

As working women, we need God. We need his answers. We need his assurance that he is with us and he will help us to stay spiritually alive as we deal with the challenges and frustrations of being on the job:

- Jennifer, a thirty-something married woman, struggles with feelings of resentment when her ideas are routinely passed on to a male coworker to develop and implement.

- Keri, an underemployed college graduate, wants to find more meaning in her job.

- Marla, a twenty-something single, longs to have a boyfriend, but doesn't want to encourage attention from non-Christian male coworkers.

- Laurie, an exhausted mom, finds that her already stretched patience is stretched even more with the complaining attitude of her cubiclemate.

- Becky, a middle-aged woman, wants to maintain friendships but wonders if everyone is too busy.

- All these women seek to have a meaningful time with God first thing in the morning and to maintain that reliance throughout the day.

Before beginning this book, I browsed and read many books for Christian working women. Though I found some very helpful ones, there was a missing element in most: the biblical perspective of a disciple's life. Some books gave good advice in many areas, then when it came to church involvement, they totally missed the boat, stating that church involvement is not always necessary in your Christian walk. They failed to knit together the composite picture of the disciple committed to God, family, work, church family and nondisciples. It's a tall order to be sure, but that's why Jesus gives us all we need to be faithful in our given circumstances:

> His divine power has given us everything we need for life and godliness through our knowledge of him who called us by his own glory and goodness. Through these he has given us his very great and precious promises, so that through them you may participate in the divine nature and escape the corruption in the world caused by evil desires (2 Peter 1:3-4).

∼

Day after day after day, life can wear us down. The twenty-four hour limit to every day, the physical limit of needing sleep, the relational limit of being "in the flesh"—all remind us that we are finite beings who are standing on our tiptoes, barely able to peek into an infinite spiritual world. It is not easy or natural to stay focused and alive spiritually. We must go against our desire to sleep in order to get focused time with God in the mornings. We must make other self-controlled decisions as we commute to work. We must be Spirit-filled to handle the temptations and irritations that are funneled our way daily at the office, the hospital, the store, the school or wherever we work. It may not be natural or easy to be a spiritual person, but it is constantly fulfilling and brings a deep-down sense of peace, joy and security...for now and for eternity.

Women have been working and living in challenging circumstances since before Jesus came, but God has had a plan in every century for disciples to be faithful. It was no easier to be a disciple in the first-century world of Chloe, Euodia, Syntyche, Tryphena and Tryphosa than today. God works with faithful hearts whatever the times and places.

What a comfort to know that the God who calls us to a righteous life—9 to 5 and 5 to 9—promises that he will give us all we need to remain *spiritually alive*. So grab your favorite mug, settle in, and pour yourself a fresh cup of life.

Sheila Jones
August 1997

Before you read further, I suggest that you look on the next page and respond to the survey that I sent out to the women quoted in the book. It will help you to focus on the areas in which you need and want the most input.

Survey for Working Women

As a working woman...

1. What is the most challenging aspect of your work life?
   guy likes me + Communication w/ Co workers

2. How do you keep your daily walk with God strong?
   What are your struggles? *No concern about my need*

3. What is your greatest challenge in maintaining friendships with disciples outside of work? How do you find
   ways to spend time with friends?

4. In thinking about your relationships at work, share
   about a time you had to deal with conflict and/or con-
   frontation.

5. While at work, what are your greatest temptations?
   Day Dream (impure) while work

6. What fears or temptations do you deal with as far as
   male coworkers are concerned? What do you do to
   make sure that these relationships stay pure? *My fear is
   guy continue to distract me.*

7. Share at least one experience of sharing your faith with
   someone at work. *Yes but not every day*

8. What is at least one way you have discovered to make
   your commute encouraging?

9. What is your greatest challenge as either a single or
   married working woman (if different from other answers above)?

10. For those who don't really like their jobs: How do you
    daily deal with your attitude? What steps are you tak-
    ing to try to find a new job?

We can either be victims of life,
time and needs, or we can take charge.
We can *decide* to start our mornings by going
to God for spiritual support.

CHAPTER 1

Hand in Hand
Daily Walk with God

Debbie stretched her arms over her head, twisted her shoulders several times and rubbed the sleep out of her right eye. *Okay. Ready for the day.* She settled into her chair at the kitchen table, took a sip of coffee and reached for her Bible and journal. The section for the day was 1 Peter 3:1-6.

Not one who is easily focused or organized, Debbie had decided several months earlier the she would no longer be tossed to and fro by her whims and emotions as she began her time with God each morning. She got a plan: She divided a book of the Bible into daily Scripture-bites. Then every day when she got up, she had a clear starting point and a clear goal: *What does this scripture say to me today? What tidbit can I carry with me throughout this day?*

She had been amazed over the past few weeks how much more focused she had been, not only in her morning times with God, but with her family and at work. "Lord," she prayed, "please don't ever let me go back to that haphazard way I was approaching my times with you each morning!"

Her husband walked in and she smiled at him. *Wow, she thought, I'm smiling, and I haven't even finished my coffee yet.* No longer would she give in to the excuse, *I'm a grouch until I have my first cup of coffee in the morning.* Maybe, just maybe, her God was more powerful than her caffeine.

❧

Early Morning Time with God

In the beginning was the Word, and the Word was with God, and the Word was God. He was with God in the beginning. Through him all things were made; without him nothing was made that has been made. In him was life, and that life was the light of men....to all who received him, to those who believed in his name, he gave the right to become children of God (John 1:1-4, 12).

God was in the beginning. Jesus was in the beginning. The Word was in the beginning. And in order for us to be spiritually alive from 9 to 5, God, Jesus and the Word need to be "in the beginning" of every day for each of us. Paul tells us that God has blessed us with "every spiritual blessing in Christ" (Ephesians 1:3). In order to be vibrant and growing and to accept those blessings, we must sink our roots deep into Jesus and into his Word:

So then, just as you received Christ Jesus as Lord, continue to live in him, rooted and built up in him, strengthened in the faith as you were taught, and overflowing with thankfulness (Colossians 2:6).

As women who are in the workforce, we are first disciples of Jesus. Our life, our breath, our meaning, our purpose, our direction, our forgiveness, our future, our relationships, our longings are all bound up in him and in our relationship with him. As the above scripture says, we should not only "receive him as Lord," we must "continue to live in him." We need to continue daily.

One woman gave these simple responses to the following questions:

> 1. How do you keep your daily walk with God strong?
> *Morning devotionals work the best.*
> 2. What are your struggles?
> *Consistency in morning devotionals.*

Doesn't that pretty well sum it up? We all know that we need time with God in the morning in order to be spiritually focused during our day. But we struggle with being consistent in the thing we need the most. That, my sisters, is a description of the spiritual battle. Paul sums it up well: "For what I want to do I do not do, but what I hate I do" (Romans 7:15). Thank God that Paul followed Romans 7 with Romans 8: "You, however, are controlled not by the sinful nature but by the Spirit, if the Spirit of God lives in you" (v. 9). Basically, the indwelling Spirit gives us the power to choose how we will spend our time and what we will focus on.

Spiritual or Religious?

One of the survey questions I asked the women was "What are your struggles in keeping your daily walk with God strong?" Here are several responses I received:

I struggle with getting up in time to have a strong relationship with God. I often have to wait till lunchtime to get my in-depth reading done. I would like to have more time to spend with God. I struggle the most with my busy schedule, feeling overwhelmed, and then going into a downward spiral because my relationship with God is not deep and reliant.

-Patti, chemist

My biggest problem is either oversleeping or falling asleep over my quiet times.

-Julie, account sales representative

I get up at 5:00 a.m. to have my quiet time before work. My struggles, of course, include just waking up!

-Diane, systems engineer

I find that I am very distracted when I am home by all the things that have to be done. ...and I can easily run around the house all morning doing stuff when what really needs to be done more than anything is my special time with God. Praying with my husband helps me be focused, helps me stop and be still.

-Sara, technical advisor

My major struggle is fighting to get up early enough to have quality time with God before leaving for work. All too often my prayers in the morning are rushed, or in the car. To fight against this, I have had to be more disciplined about getting to bed on time.

-Lisa, educational support/software company

It doesn't really matter what we do or what our schedule is or how old we are, all of us have to make the decision that we will get time with God every day. Life has a way of pushing itself in on us. Time has a way of pressing us. Needs have a way of pressuring us.

We can either be victims of life, time and needs, or we can take charge. We can *decide* to start our mornings by going to God for spiritual support and by imitating his mind-set, and we can do it!

How many times have we asked a Christian friend, "How is your morning time with God every day?" and she replies, "Not that great. It's just so hard to find the time." Somehow, when I personally respond like that, it makes perfect sense, and I excuse my lack of focus and spirituality. But when I hear it from someone else, it hits me between the eyes. I am not down on any of my friends, because I have done the same thing, but it makes me realize that when we make statements like this, we are admitting that we are not dependent on God. We are actually dependent upon ourselves. A truly desperate person finds time to pray, to ask for help, to connect with God daily…just like a hungry person finds time to eat.

As a child I remember singing, "You gotta walk that lonesome valley / You gotta walk it by yourself / Nobody else can walk it for you / You gotta walk it by yourself." That is the way it is in spending time with God as adults. Nobody else can get up early for you. Nobody else can determine that you will depend upon God. Nobody else can pray in your place. You gotta do it by yourself.

Down deep in our character, we must answer the question, "Am I spiritual or am I religious?" The spiritual woman is intense about getting time with God because she knows she desperately needs it—she relies on God. The religious woman is casual about getting time with God because she doesn't really believe she needs it—she relies on herself.

Make It Happen

One of my daughters at seventeen was bemoaning the fact that she has such a rough time waking up in the morning. She was feeling defeated because she did not see herself changing. She was not having consistent times with God daily, even though she had repented and had resolved to be different. My suggestion to her was to put into practice the concept embodied in Ephesians 3:20:

> Now to him who is able to do immeasurably more than all we ask or imagine, according to his power that is at work within us, to him be glory in the church and in Christ Jesus throughout all generations, for ever and ever! Amen.

That is, *imagine it happening.* Sometimes we don't change because we never even allow ourselves to imagine what we would be like if we did change. God gave us our imaginations for a purpose—to inspire us to *do* and to *be* more than we are. Unfortunately, we allow Satan to use our imaginations to tempt us more often than we allow God to use them to inspire us. Paul (and the Holy Spirit) says that God "is able to do immeasurably more than all we ask or imagine."

So, I told my daughter that she would never change what she could not even imagine. I asked her to imagine the alarm going off and then to see herself hitting the alarm button and jumping out of bed. She groaned and said she couldn't do it. I reminded her, "If you won't even let yourself believe long enough to imagine it, you will never believe or accept that you can change this in your character."

After a few minutes of gentle, but firm, coaxing, we went

through the whole scenario several times (with alarm sound effects and all). *Ring-g-g-g-g-g-g! Hit the "off" button! Jump out of bed!* After a few practice runs, she was more ready than ever to believe that God has the power to change even a sleepyhead like her.

Do you need to do some repenting, some imagining, some praying, some changing? You have everything you need for life and godliness in Christ Jesus. You can be consistent in your times with God! Stop doubting, and believe! Say Yes to God!

Perhaps it would help us if we imagined Jesus standing beside our beds and saying the same thing he said to his disciples: "Why are you sleeping? Get up and pray so that you will not fall into temptation" (Luke 22:46).

Say No to Legalism

"But some mornings are challenging. Things beyond my control cut out my special time with God. Then my whole day is ruined." Have you ever thought or said something like this? Once and for all we have got to stop having a legalistic view of our "quiet time." It is not an *it!* We shouldn't ask each other, "Have you had *it* today?" or "Are you having *them* regularly?" The question is, "Are you close to God?" or "Are you having meaningful times communicating with God?"

I have known people who do penance all day because they did not get a certain amount of time with God that morning. They feel that God is not with them, so they would rather just get that day over with and start a new day, making sure they start with a quiet time. They don't really look for God to use them in someone's life that day, and they feel guilty about praying for help when tempted. They operate out of a doghouse mentality, simply looking forward to getting out of the doghouse the next day when they perform well enough. This may seem exaggerated to some of us, but I am convinced it is true.

God is not interested in our punching our quiet-time cards. He is interested in our sharing our hearts with him. He is not interested in our getting our Bible reading in. He is interested in sharing his heart with us. Some will probably say to him on that day, "Lord, Lord, did I not have a quiet time every day?" And he will say to them "Yes, you had a quiet time, but you never really gave me your heart. You never trusted me to give mine to you. Therefore, I don't know you."

We should plan to have special time communing with God before the hustle and bustle of the day pulls and distracts us. But if a sick child or a call from a coworker asking for a ride cuts our time short, we must remember that our relationship with God is ongoing; it is not defined by the length or quality of our "quiet time" on any certain day. In situations such as those mentioned, I choose to focus on a specific verse—even if I just pull it up from memory: "My God will meet all your needs according to his glorious riches in Christ Jesus" (Philippians 4:19). Or "Do not be anxious about anything, but in everything, by prayer and petition, with thanksgiving, present your requests to God" (Philippians 4:6). Or "The only thing that counts is faith expressing itself through love" (Galatians 5:6). Any of these, or hundreds of others, can help us get our direction and focus for the day. We can then use our energy and the little time we do have to focus on God and his commands and his promises instead of bemoaning, and even complaining about, the lack of time we have. Remember, we are always with God and he is always with us (Matthew 28:20).

It should go without saying, but I will say it anyway (moms are like that, you know!): Our goal and expectation should always be to have specific, special, meaningful time with God every morning. It's like the Israelites and the manna. Moses told them to gather manna every morning, but to gather just enough for that day. This helped the people to remember that they were dependent upon God.

> He humbled you, causing you to hunger and then feeding you with manna, which neither you nor your fathers had known, to teach you that man does not live on bread alone but on every word that comes from the mouth of the LORD (Deuteronomy 8:3).

If they gathered extra manna so they could sleep in the next day, the manna rotted, became infested with maggots and began to smell. Yuck!

In the same way, we should have a mind-set of gathering fresh spiritual food every day—enough for that day. (As Jesus said in Matthew 6:34, "Each day has enough trouble of its own.") But over the Sabbath, they were not to gather manna, and that which they had gathered the day before stayed fresh. So it is that there are times every once in a while that we aren't able to gather new manna, but, by grace, what we have already gathered feeds us that day. We would not want to depend on eating stored manna though, because we would find the spiritual maggots of complacency and apathy eating away at our zeal and our understanding of God's word.

Say No to Self-Sufficiency

I tend to be self-sufficient. How about you? What is your first thought when you open your eyes in the morning? Is it, *Morning, already?* or *Where's the snooze button?* or *One-two-three...and then I'll get up?* Or is it something more spiritual in nature?

My husband, Tom, has multiple sclerosis. He has made me aware that the first thought of those who are physically challenged is often something along these lines: *Am I going to be able to get up today? God, please help me!* or *I slept all night, but I still feel like a truck ran over me. There's no way for me to get going without God today.* They realize immediately that they will need God in order to get out of bed and to get ready for their day. When I first wake up, I do not naturally think about how much I need God. I simply jump out of bed, after waiting as long as I can, and go full force into getting ready for my day. The arrogance of my approach to a new day staggers me. Do I have to have a physical challenge to realize that I am totally dependent on God for each breath I take?

I decided to train myself to think upon waking, *Without God I cannot be a spiritual person today. I cannot be like Jesus. No chance. I am totally dependent on him.* I am still not perfect in my early morning response, but I am more aware than I once was of my immediate need for God as I start my day. The Scriptures are full of reminders not to trust in ourselves:

> Woe to those who go down to Egypt for help,
>   who rely on horses,
> who trust in the multitude of their chariots
>   and in the great strength of their horsemen,
> but do not look to the Holy One of Israel
>   or seek help from the LORD (Isaiah 31:1).

> This is what the LORD says:
> "Cursed is the one who trusts in man,
>   who depends on flesh for his strength
>   and whose heart turns away from the LORD.
> But blessed is the man who trusts in the LORD,
>   whose confidence is in him" (Jeremiah 17:5, 7).

It is obvious that self-sufficiency is not a twentieth- or twenty-first-century thing. It is simply a human thing!

Gwendellyn, a twenty-two-year-old actuary says,

> Being gut-level real (with God and myself) is a challenge because I have so many different responsibilities now that I'm "on my own." I can tend to take them all on myself and leave God out of the loop.

If we make a loop and leave God out of it, we can easily hang ourselves in it. And great is the choke thereof!

What do you want your first thought to be when you open your eyes? Decide. Then train yourself in godliness. Grab hold of God and his power when you first wake up. You will certainly need to tighten your grip as your day unfolds.

Getting Specific

We've all done the what-am-I-going-to-read-this-morning thing, haven't we? *Where's my Bible? Where's my notebook? Now, what do I want to read?* Thumb, thumb, thumb. *What does that mean? Oh well, never mind. Here's something.* Read, read, read. *Now, what did I read? Maybe I'd better choose another passage…oh my, time has flown. I'd better pray and then start getting dressed.*

Not too satisfying or fulfilling, is it? Sometimes we eat our spiritual breakfast in much the same way that we eat our physical breakfast—on the run. Drive-through spirituality doesn't feed the soul! Three words are crucial to the everyday life of a working woman: planning, planning and planning. We must be purposeful in our choices. "Spontaneity" is sometimes used as a euphemism for "disorganization" or "laziness." When we don't plan, we get frustrated. As much as we would like it to be true that we can grab life on the run without it grabbing us back, it simply is not.

Responding to the question about her daily times with God, one woman said,

> I feel a lot more motivated when I have specific direction. Lately I've been reading Psalms and Proverbs and writing down ones that apply to my character so when I struggle with criticalness, I can go to my "critical" page. When I struggle with insecurity and fear, I can go to that page in my journal or notebook. This really helps me.

In the area of our ongoing Bible study, we need to take enough time to plan what we want to learn, what we want to accomplish and how we want to grow. Those who grow spiritually are those who take the time to plan and who execute the plan.

I have been inconsistent myself over the years in this area: Sometimes I have been right on target, studying a biblical book or a topic. Other times I have been treading water in my study times. It all goes back to how much I realize that I need God. If I am allowing self-sufficiency in my life, my study times show it. I can be standing on one foot, ready to get going in my day because I have so much to do…on my own. How much better it is when I plan, stop, focus and apply.

During the Day

So far, we have discussed the importance of getting our hearts and minds set at the beginning of our workdays. How about staying focused all day long? How do we maintain a spiritual mind-set throughout the day? Let's see how some women do it:

> Having a daily memory scripture helps. Expressing personal convictions or opinions to coworkers helps keep me accountable to my standard.
>
> *-Charlene, marketing associate*

> Sometimes I have to go to the bathroom to pray during the day when I get frustrated or if I see something in someone's character (or my own character). I'll go in the bathroom to pray for them and also ask God to help me encourage them.
>
> *-Leslie, research assistant*

> I definitely need time with God in the morning. I also go into the ladies room to pray and practice "letting go" of anxiety as soon as it comes along.
>
> *-Lara, manager of information/graphic design firm*

Another thing I'll sometimes do is go for a walk at lunch down this quiet tree-lined street near our office building, and I'll make myself look at the things God made.... *Oh, God made that sky and the clouds and that tree over there and that little bird and those people up there.* If I don't focus my thoughts that way, sometimes walking can be filled up with looking at the cars parked on the street, the lovely houses and lawns or the clothes people are wearing, and I miss the point entirely.

-*Sara, technical advisor*

I have another disciple on my job, and we encourage each other a lot! Also, I have to just take a walk sometimes and pray.

-*Julie, account sales representative*

I leave my office at the height of tension and pray in the bathroom, or go for a quick walk or call a disciple to encourage them or get help.

-*Gina, special programs coordinator*

I'm certain that not too many prayers rise to God from corporate boardrooms. I am just as certain that *many* prayers rise to God from corporate bathrooms. Jesus instructed his followers,

"But when you pray, go into your room, close the door and pray to your Father, who is unseen. Then your Father, who sees what is done in secret, will reward you" (Matthew 6:6).

The King James version of the Bible says we are to enter the "closet" and pray. It would seem that the bathroom is the "closet" of the working woman.

Besides bathroom prayers, the other common denominator of workday praying seems to be walks. Getting away from the whole scene and being focused on God is refreshing. Several of the people in my office go to a nearby cemetery to pray and to be out in nature during lunch. Of course, in New England this is not a year-round activity.

Scripture plaques or screen savers serve as reminders to some. Certainly our offices should not resemble the plaque section of a Christian bookstore, but subtle statements enable coworkers to know that we are relying on God. Those who are spiritually minded will possibly be drawn to us since they know that we are not ashamed of making a statement about our faith.

Quick calls here and there to other disciples, asking them to pray for specific situations, is certainly encouraging. It is incredibly important, though, not to abuse this privilege. When at work, we are paid to work, not to counsel or have lengthy ministry conversations or to study the Bible with people. Above all, we must have integrity in our time-usage. (We will discuss time-usage thoroughly in Chapter 4.)

One sister summed up all of these tactics (and added at least one more) in her thorough response:

> Besides having quiet times on subjects that I may be struggling with (staying righteous when mistreated, not being anxious when there are deadlines and there is not enough time to do everything I need to do, etc.), I have devotional books and Bibles in my office, so during a break, I can look at scriptures. I also have software on my computer system which scrolls scriptures across the screen or produces a text file of scriptures. I also listen to spiritual music at work (walkman). My office has little plaques with

scriptures as well. All these things help. Then there is the trip to the bathroom just to pray when days are really rough. I can send E-mail out to other disciples when I am struggling or just having a difficult day. Also, at times I take a walk during lunch time just to pray.

-*Alice, software engineer*

A Godly Example

Have you ever thought of Nehemiah as being a godly example to you during your workday? His occupation was that of cupbearer to King Artaxerxes. Generally, the cupbearer was a trusted employee of the king. His specific job was to taste the wine from the cup out of which the king would drink since poisoning was the weapon of choice for assassins.

After receiving the disheartening news that the wall of Jerusalem had been destroyed and that the exiles who had returned were in trouble and disgrace, Nehemiah was brokenhearted. He mourned and fasted and poured out his heart to God. Then, when it was time for him to "go to work," he prayed for his communication and his relationship with his employer: "Give your servant success today by granting him favor in the presence of this man" (Nehemiah 1:11). Nehemiah was then honest with the king when asked why he was sad; he was willing to be real and personal in a business setting. Then we see him maintaining his spiritual focus as he prayed on the job and on the spot:

> The king said to me, "What is it you want?"
> Then I prayed to the God of heaven, and I answered the king, "If it pleases the king and if your servant has found favor in

his sight, let him send me to the city in Judah where my fathers
are buried so that I can rebuild it" (2:4-5).

Whether we are asking for time off (as Nehemiah was doing),
asking about information for a report that is due or trying to resolve a conflict, we should "pray to the God of heaven" and then
"answer" or speak or explain.

Even though I work in an all-Christian setting at DPI, I still
find myself getting into my writing, my editing, my mail-answer-
ing, my whatever without being mindful of God. Having a spiritual mind-set all day long is a challenge when we are focusing our
mind-power on tasks at hand. That's why, like Nehemiah, we need
to pray before going to the job and pray while on the job to be
successful for God in every interaction, in every task, in every
meeting. We must do battle with self-reliance; it is our enemy, not
our friend.

⌐๑

It is God's desire to help us to stay at peace during stressful
times, in the shadow of looming deadlines, in the midst of office
tension and in the wake of office politics:

> You will keep in perfect peace
> him whose mind is steadfast,
> because he trusts in you (Isaiah 26:3).

"In the beginning" of each day, look to God. Throughout each
day "pray to the God of heaven." And trust that he will be with you
not only to the end of the day, but to the "very end of the age"
(Matthew 28:20).

A Fresh Cup of Life

How would you describe your early morning times with God? *Take time to read slowly but the same time I have problem w/distance*

Do you currently have a plan for what you will study daily? If not, when will you get one? *Yes, I study about relationships in between my job and God.*

How did you grow in your convictions as a result of reading this chapter? *Set on focus about plans*

What specifics did you learn that you want to put into practice? *I need to practice on my courage to pray in bathroom or wherever.*

During your workday, what do you do to maintain a spiritual focus?

God is a God who says yes to all the should-be-done's. He never asks anything of us that he does not give us the power or opportunity to do.

CHAPTER 2

❧

People
Who Need People

Maintaining Friendships

She felt lonely, really lonely. Sure, it was the day before her period, and that accounted for some of what she was feeling. But she realized that lately the feeling seldom left her—it only got more intense or less intense depending on her hormone level.

Jennifer was a disciple; she was committed to Jesus and to his church. She did all the things she was supposed to do: She attended all the services and special events. She got together with her discipleship partners weekly. She prayed with her husband most days. She had daily quiet times with God. So, when the gnawing loneliness pressed in on her, she was perplexed. She was so blessed. Many people genuinely cared about her. Why was she lonely? What was she lonely for?

She thought back to her single days. She remembered staying up until all hours talking and sharing her life, her heart. The very thought made her feel less lonely and then more lonely. Was that it? Sharing her life, her heart? Her schedule had become so hectic: marriage, meals, upkeep of the house, leading a discipleship group, work, workout time, etc. She ran from person to person, from thing to thing, from activity to activity. In all her running, she realized that she seldom took the time to stop and think about and share what she was thinking and feeling. She had lost her emotional connection to other people.

That thought was encouraging, though. If something is lost, it can generally be found. Lost is one thing; destroyed is another. Her emotional connection was not destroyed; it was simply lost.

⁓

"People who need people / are the luckiest people in the world." If Barbra Streisand is right about this, and she is, we are *all* very lucky people. We do need other people. "Friendship" is one of the warmest words in the English language. Jennifer, in the story above, was simply realizing how much she needed people in her life. A full and busy life is not necessarily fulfilling: Relationships are. God made us this way. No wonder the Bible includes so many "one-another" passages: Love one another, confess to one another, pray for one another, correct one another, etc. We were made to be in relationship with God and with each other. God himself embodies relationship; though being "one" he is "three": the Father, the Son and the Holy Spirit. Because he is relational himself, he teaches us how to deal with the loneliness we sometimes feel and how to build fulfilling relationships.

Was Jesus Ever Lonely?

Have you ever wondered if Jesus experienced loneliness? The Hebrews writer tells us that he was "tempted in every way, just as we are" (4:15). Surely that means that he felt every emotion that we feel. The Son of God…lonely and needing friends? Let's consider some situations in which that could have been the case.

Jesus and Others

Have you ever known a child who was more mature in his conceptual thinking than other children his age? While in the sixth grade, I can remember my sister writing poetry that dealt with emotional and relational concepts that were beyond most kids her age. In fact, the teacher talked with my mother about her concern that Emily was depressed. She actually wasn't depressed; she just thought deeply for an eleven-year-old. How much more would Jesus have felt different from the boys around him? He was conversing with and amazing the elders in the temple when he was only twelve years old! Although he grew in wisdom and knowledge and in favor with God and man, it's quite possible that he felt isolated at times from his playmates.

When he was tempted in the desert, he was by himself. No earthly friend stood beside him, praying for him and supporting him. No one had any idea what he was experiencing. He did spiritual battle with the attendance of only his Father, Satan and the angels. For forty days he was alone, fighting the definitive fight of his spiritual life, setting the course for his path to the cross. All this going on and no human friend understood.

What about the crowds? Any public figure will tell you, if he or she is honest, that the crowds do not meet your need for true acceptance and understanding and love. You cannot have a reciprocal relationship that meets mutual needs with a fickle crowd of people who simply want to get their needs met in some way through you. The crowds went from yelling "Hosanna" to yelling "Crucify him" within a span of a few days.

How about the leaders in his life? Spiritual leaders are to "be there" for us when we need guidance and understanding. He had looked up to them and learned from them when he was a boy, but what about when he became a man? The gospel accounts make it clear: They had no fondness in their hearts for him. As he spoke secrets from the God they professed to worship, they scorned him, hated him, were jealous of him and tried to trap him in every God-drenched word he spoke. Friendship and support? I don't think so.

Jesus had his purpose on straight as he lived in the shadow of his own cross. He knew his God-given destiny and he stepped in the path of it daily. But did anyone understand? Did anyone ever say, "Jesus, I respect and appreciate you so much for choosing to do God's will. I know you are here to give your life as a ransom for all of us. You are doing what is right. Do not allow anything or anyone to deter you. I will be praying for you to remain faithful"? Yes, some men did speak with him this way, but as far as I can tell from reading the Gospels, only once did it happen. And those friends had to be brought back from the dead!

He had spoken these words eight days before he met with Moses and Elijah on the top of the mountain:

"The Son of Man must suffer many things and be rejected by the elders, chief priests and teachers of the law, and he must be killed and on the third day be raised to life" (Luke 9:22).

How much more alone might someone feel? I believe Jesus needed encouragement. He needed to hear from others who had been given a mission by God, a mission that took them down lonely roads and elicited rejection from people. Luke tells us that Moses and Elijah "appeared in glorious splendor, talking with Jesus. They spoke about his departure, which he was about to bring to fulfillment at Jerusalem" (Luke 9:31). They understood what God had called him to. They encouraged him. They helped him to prepare spiritually for the grueling task ahead. Their coming was a gracious gift from a Father who loved him. Their presence must have reminded him, "I am not alone, for my Father is with me" (John 16:32).

Add to the mix the betrayal of Judas, one of his prayer-picked twelve, and the denial of Peter, one of his closest friends in the world. What an arrow of pain must have pierced his heart of love to hear from the lips of his friend, "I don't know the man"…and to hear those words coarsely edged with curses that slapped the face of God, the God Jesus had daily poured himself out to help Peter know.

Then, finally, see him on the cross. Feel his pain as the Father who loved him so very much turned his back on him in his time of greatest need, causing him to cry out with the Psalmist, "My God, my God, why have you forsaken me?"

Did Jesus feel loneliness? I think he did. Otherwise, why would he have taken his three closest friends with him to Gethsemane? But never once did he allow loneliness to cause him to sin. Never once did he give in to his own need to be understood and thus, neglect to understand others. He kept his focus on God and on meeting the needs of others.

How sweet it must have been when he talked with his disciples after the resurrection, and they finally understood.

I have a special place in my heart for Mary, Martha and Lazarus. Is it any wonder that Jesus' visits at the house of these friends in Bethany were frequent and refreshing? If anyone on earth had an inkling of the sacrifice that Jesus was about to make, I think it was Mary. After she lavishly anointed his head with oil, he said,

> "She did what she could. She poured perfume on my body be-forehand to prepare for my burial. I tell you the truth, wherever the gospel is preached throughout the world, what she has done will also be told, in memory of her" (Mark 14:8-9).

I'm thankful she and her brother and sister were friends to Jesus.

The Message to Us

What does an understanding of the loneliness of Jesus say to us as women at the turn of the twentieth century? What does it say when we are feeling lonely and apart from others in our hearts? It says that feeling lonely is not necessarily a bad thing. It reminds us that we need God and we need other people. We were not made to live alone. It also says that when we are lonely, we need to turn to God, and we need to initiate meeting the needs of others. We are not to fall into self-pity and fill ourselves up with self-centeredness, whining about other people not meeting our needs or not initiating closeness with us.

It also says that no person will ultimately meet our deepest needs; only God can. And because Jesus died for us and experienced the rejection that should have been ours, God will always be with us. He will never turn his back on us. But Jesus wants so much to meet our need for understanding on this earth, that he pulls together a group to support, help, encourage and understand each other as we seek to accomplish his mission. We don't have to wait for people to be brought back from the dead to understand us. We have his body, the church.

In imitating his Lord, Paul tells the Thessalonians that "he lived among them for their sake." He learned well from the Master Discipler. He did not dwell on his need for understanding or acceptance or love; instead, he gave to, understood and accepted others. And in the process they became very dear to his heart. He was not a sad, self-focused man; he had friendships that meant the world to him—Aquila, Priscilla, Timothy, Luke and others.

Feelings of loneliness will come. In fact, a certain vestige of loneliness will always nestle in our hearts; we will not fully be at rest until we are in the actual presence of God. This is what Paul means when he says, "Meanwhile we groan, longing to be clothed with our heavenly dwelling" (2 Corinthians 5:2). Accept it. When you feel lonely, read the Psalms. David and other psalmists speak candidly about their feelings of loneliness. Then they remind themselves of truth: God loves me and he is with me. Hold on to their Holy Spirit-inspired words and those of other biblical writers. And decide to do what Jesus and Paul did: Give your love away and live among others for their sake. You will be filled with the fresh cup of life God meant for you to have. And you will find the emotional connection through which God blesses us…closeness to him and to others. Remember that Jesus told us, "Whoever loses his life for me will find it" (Matthew 16:25).

Friendships with Disciples

But how can you work full time and maintain relationships with disciples? God wants it to be done. He wants us to love and support each other. He wants us to have meaningful, close friendships. It should be done, but can it be done? God is a God who says yes to all the should-be-done's. He never asks anything of us that he does not give us the power or opportunity to do.

We might also note that Jennifer, in our beginning story, was happy in her marriage to her husband, Jeff. He was her best friend. But even if you are happily married, you still need to be sharing your heart with other women. As wonderful as your husband is, he is not able to meet all of your emotional needs, and you should not rely on him to do so. Other women can help you understand yourself and can challenge you in a special way that only they can do.

How Can It Happen?

We've all seen the little soft-touch books...the ones with pastel hues...a picture of two cups of coffee or tea...a basket of muffins...a fresh bouquet of daisies to the side. You don't see the people, but obviously, one woman has lovingly prepared for another to visit. The picture speaks of friendship, of sharing, of warmth, of belonging. It says, "Slow down. Take time to be with your friend. Don't rush out to an appointment. Stay and enjoy being together."

Somehow, it feels good just to think about this relaxing and reassuring scene. But how does it match up with your life? Do you have many of those moments with friends? Does anybody really have them? Are they mythical, drummed up by advertising agencies and book publishers to sell us the mistaken idea that if we buy a product or a book, we will have friendship, sharing, warmth, belonging?

Certainly, in our fast- and even frantic-paced world, such tranquil, unruffled times with a friend do seem a luxury, a remote possibility. I fear that the scene might realistically look a little more like this:

Maggie: Judy, hi! It's Maggie. It's been months since we just sat down and talked with each other. With both of us working full time now, I hardly see you anymore. Why don't you stop by Saturday morning for coffee?

Judy: Oh, Maggie, I would love to! I miss being with you. But Saturday morning doesn't work very well for me. Peter has Little League practice, and

Sarah has her first dance recital. Stan and I are splitting up to cover both bases.

Maggie: Maybe lunch then?

Judy: I wish, but honestly, my laundry is reaching flood-level proportions. If I don't stay home the rest of the day and go after it, Monday morning will be mutinous around here. My kids can only turn their underwear inside out one time without my feeling really guilty! (laughs)

Maggie: Sunday afternoon?

Judy: My discipleship group is getting together to plan a shower for one of our members then. How about meeting me at Starbucks later in the evening?

Maggie: No, that won't work for me. I committed myself to be at home to help Bill with filing bills and stuff *and* to have some romantic time before we are too exhausted...Oh, well, it was a good idea anyway. I'll see you at church in the morning...maybe our families can sit together at least.

Judy: Well, we have some visitors coming with us. They already know the Martins, so we were going to try to sit with them. But, I love you and I want to get to be with you. Maybe we can just meet for lunch at a halfway point during the week.

Maggie: No...won't work. I only have thirty minutes for lunch since I opted to get off thirty minutes early to get more time with my kids. Getting together was a good idea, but I guess we just can't work it out any time soon. I love you, though!

The coffee cups stay in the cupboard. The Pillsbury muffins are still in the box. The flowers are unpicked or unbought. A relaxing time together for these two friends remains in the thought and imagination stage.

I paint this picture not to discourage us as working women (and especially working mothers), but rather, to depict reality. We must clearly understand and define the facts before we can work on finding solutions. In order to do that, though, we must first accept our "givens."

As disciples who want to keep learning and growing and sharing, we need time with other disciples. That's a given. As working women, we are not able to go out for coffee during the day together or take our kids to the McDonald's playground or to the park. That's also a given. Accept it. Don't fight it, bemoan it or blame anyone for it. Here are some ideas to help:

1. Define and accept your givens.

Some of my basic givens are:
- I have to work.
- I must do laundry and clean my house.
- My husband has MS, and therefore, I have extra responsibilities around the house.
- When I get in at night, I need to fix a good dinner.
- I need to maintain my relationship with my husband—emotionally, spiritually and sexually.
- My last daughter at home needs my time and attention, as do my other two.
- My energy is somewhat depleted because of my recent surgery.

- I often have meetings, individual Bible studies or counseling sessions in the evening.
- I am discipling several women with whom I want to spend time every week.
- I also want to be with my friend who disciples me.

Stop and think. What are your givens? Do you accept these givens? Are you willing to be content "in any and every situation" as Paul was? Do you need to pray more about it and become content? If so, I suggest a good study of Philippians 4:4-13.

2. Be positive and creative in finding ways to spend time with other disciples and ways to stay connected during the week.

Let's ask some other working women how they do it:

Mostly the time I get to spend with other disciples is having quiet times together and discipleship times on the weekends.

-Diane, systems engineer, married with no children

My son and I try to have dinner with others. Since we have to eat anyway, we might as well eat with others and get to spend time with them that way!

-Ann, software engineer, single mom

Leslie and I see each other for leaders' meeting once a week, but we are busy with "business," so I say (maybe every three or four months) on a Monday, "Don't plan anything. I'm coming over to fix dinner, and we'll watch a movie and stay up and talk till midnight." Then we'll get up and have a great quiet time. Leslie and I love to pray, so we'll pray two or three times throughout the night—like ten to thirty minutes each session."

-Cindy, technical recruiter, single

I try to have lunches a lot and coffee after work when I can. I love E-mail and make phone calls often when I'm cooking dinner, before my husband gets home. We also plan a lot of dates with other couples on Friday or Saturday nights to keep up and develop other friendships.

-Julie, account sales representative, married with no children

I try to make my phone calls while I'm cooking or while I'm cleaning the kitchen. As a working mom, I'm continually trying to do two, or even three, things at once to try to save time.

-professional (no specific occupation given), married with children

I have to work on discipline with my schedule and sticking to my schedule. I am naturally a fly-by-the-seat-of-my-pants sort of gal, but I have learned to be more organized with my life.

-Lara, manager of information/graphic design company, single

Weekly devotional time with discipler happens before work.

-Charlotte, sequence integration engineer, married with children

My challenge is coordinating my schedule and then sticking to it. It is so easy to take too much extra time to do nothing.... When I can find five minutes I use it to make a call.

-Alisa, customer service representative, married with no children

Since I am not able to go home between work and midweek service, I always use that time to get with someone. Often I get with a particular sister who was in my wedding, but who is now in a different sector of the church. We travel to midweek together. All we do is ride the subway together, but somehow it is such a special time.

-Sara, senior project leader, married with no children

The greatest challenge is time and sheer fatigue. As a single, I would go out to dinner, coffee, movies, the gym, etc. with other single professionals. We could be very spontaneous and plan these outings at 4:30 p.m. As a working mother of three children, I have to plan, literally, weeks in advance.
-*Suzanne, engineer, married with children*

I manage my time by first seeking advice on my weekly schedule from women who have a lot of responsibilities and are still effective.... I wake up at 5:15 and pray with a sister, or someone I'm studying with, over the phone. We pray for fifteen minutes.
-*Marcie, executive secretary/federal government, single mom*

Take a few minutes to glance back over the responses from women of different ages and different life situations. What themes do you see emerging?

Here are some that I see:
- Use small amounts of time wisely and relationally.
- Plan!
- Things that you normally have to do anyway, do with others.
- Do several or at least a couple of things at one time.
- Be determined.
- Sacrifice to get time with others.
- Make sure you have some spiritually focused times with others.
- Just hang out sometimes and relax.
- Don't rely on getting together physically—
  communicate more consistently through phone or E-mail.
- Use "dead" time to full advantage.

3. Make Special Times Happen

Going back to the earlier picture of the muffins, the flowers, tea or coffee for two:...don't think this can never happen in your life. You can have extra-special times every once in a while. Consider the following plan of action:

1. Write down a list of friends you want to be able to spend some time with, possibly ones you do not see very often. Accept that you will not spend a lot of time with each of these, so you will not be discouraged or disappointed when considering the list.

2. Prioritize (not a popularity contest, just deciding, for whatever reasons, which ones you want or need to see first).

3. Consider the next month's scheduled activities. Find several possible times to get with this friend. Call her and set a time before she has scheduled all available time slots. (The early bird gets the time slot, you know!) Do this each month with a different friend—maybe even plan two months in advance.

4. Plan to make the time special: gourmet coffee and biscotti…in or out…or Saturday luncheon at a neat little place you have discovered…or afternoon tea. Maybe you would want to bring a meaningful card to give to your friend.

5. Pray before you get together, asking God to help you use the time in the very best way. Think of one way you have grown spiritually, and think of one encouraging comment you want to make to your friend.

6. Remember that a special time like this with a friend can help you to stay in each other's heart even though you are not together often.

You may react and say, "Friendship times should be more spontaneous." That's all well and good. It would be awesome if they could be, and actually, God does bless us here and there with a serendipity friendship time. But if we complain about lack of spontaneity, we could be complaining a year from now...and still not have made time to be with some of our friends. So, just accept that this is where we as working women are, and be positive in looking for solutions. The least encouraging thing you could do is to finally get some time with someone and spend most of it bemoaning the fact that you do not get more! If you have a positive, faith-filled attitude, God will multiply your time as he did the loaves and fishes, and it will seem that you got even more than you did—emotionally and spiritually.

As Browning said, "Ah, but a man's reach would exceed his grasp, / Or what's a heaven for?"[1] If we were able to have all the time with all the people anytime we wanted, how would heaven be distinctive? We are bound by our humanity. We can only be in one place at one time. We can only give total attention to one person at one time. In fact, the same was true for Jesus. He chose to bind himself with flesh. He chose to limit himself to being able to communicate only with a select number of people while on this earth.

Someday our capacity to give to and to be with others will be multiplied to mindboggling proportions, just as Jesus' ability is. But for now, we must be content with what we have and thank

[1] from "Andrea del Sarto" by Robert Browning

God for it. Each friendship and each time spent with a friend is a foretaste of the all-encompassing unity and connection we will feel to everyone in heaven.

Friendships at Work

In Chapter 5 we will discuss sharing our faith at work, and in Chapter 7 we will talk more about being a team player in our relationships at work. Here, I simply want to make the point that in building friendships at work, we must live out biblical principles and yet not expect our coworkers to live out those same principles. Sometimes when we interact with non-Christian friends, we expect them to respond as Christians would; and we get frustrated, angry and confused when they don't. Once we accept the fact that we do not share a common standard with nondisciples, we can get down to being an example of unconditional love. Through that love we can draw them to Jesus, which is our purpose in their lives.

Enjoy work friends! Laugh with them; share little things that happen in your day; cry with them when they hurt; give them small gifts, such as their favorite candy bar (or piece of fruit!). And don't be afraid to learn from them. Even though they may not be Christians, they can teach us many things through their experiences, talents and character strengths. They can help us change our character if we ask them. For example, if we tend to be late to work, we can ask a coworker who is always on time, "How do you do it?" Sometimes we are too afraid just to be friends because we think we should be perfect or the best in every area. Who wants a friend like that? I sure wouldn't be fired up about it!

One woman shared about how important her work friends were in her life:

> My friends at work were the bright spot for me in my previous job. I worked with thirty other women as a customer service representative for a retail catalog company. Dealing with irate customers and a fast-paced environment can be challenging, especially when the company is also in Chapter 11 and layoffs/downsizing are the result. One of my friends there refused to let her spirits be dampened by our environment. I learned a lot from her about lightening up and not taking myself and my job so seriously. Her great sense of humor and friendliness really made a difference. We would slap post-it notes with smiley faces on each other's computers after particularly difficult phone conversations. I think it's important as a disciple to not only be a friend and a giver, but to allow others to be friends and givers to us as well!
>
> *-Lisa, editorial assistant*

A note of caution though: Because of the day-in and day-out physical and emotional partnership in achieving a goal or completing a project, we can begin to be more emotionally attached to our work family than we are to the body of Christ. It feels good to be part of the group, to have a common purpose, to feel like we belong. Each work environment becomes its own little world with its own schedules, peeves, frustrations, joys and victories. While being relatable and giving our best at work, we should always guard against being more connected to our work friends than to our Christian friends. If we allow this to happen, we will become less spiritual and less kingdom-oriented in our thinking. We will dilute the message of Jesus and become weak in our own convictions.

Keep a vision of your workmates becoming friends with whom you can share on a deeper level. Look to God to help you be a friend to them by being compassionate, by listening, by affirming, by looking to meet their needs, and by being open to learning from them.

&

As working women, celebrate your friendships with other women. Deal with loneliness in a righteous way. Pray that God will enable you to find time to give your heart to friends every day of your life. Make the decision to be real and open with God, so that realness and openness is right on the top of your heart—ready to be given quickly to your friends throughout the day. Accept your givens and grow in your giving!

A Fresh Cup of Life

Look over the story at the beginning of the chapter. Do you identify with any of Jennifer's feelings of loneliness? If so, what strategies has this chapter given you to help overcome these feelings?

If you didn't already make a list of the "givens" in your life, do it now. Are you content with these givens? If not, how will you go about becoming content?

What did you learn from the chapter that will help you build your friendships with other disciples?

How would you describe your friendships at work?

Which biblical principles do you apply to your friendships at work on an ongoing basis?

Do you find ways to enjoy work friends? Are you willing to be real with them and to ask them for help in areas of your life? If so, how have they helped you to grow? If not, how can you grow in these friendships?

Jesus was not only a *man* of integrity;
Jesus *was* integrity.

CHAPTER 3

❧

Integrity on the Job
Part One — Integrity of Speech

She glanced around the office, looking for a place to hide. Any place. Under the desk? No, that would look really stupid if he found her there. What would she say, "I lost my contact"? She didn't even wear contacts. And the whole reason she wanted to hide was because she did not want to lie. So she couldn't lie about why she was under the desk either. As she thought of the possible scene, *I Love Lucy* came to mind, and she chuckled out loud. She could just see Lucy Ricardo under a desk, her eyes wide with the fear of being caught.

Buzz-z-z-z-z!!! *Karen, could you come in please?*

As Mr. Logan's administrative assistant, Karen kept up with every detail of his work-life, and even some details of his nonwork-life: flowers to his wife on their anniversary, birthday gifts to his daughter, checkbook balancing. But one thing she refused to do was to lie for him. And she knew that he was calling her into his office to ask her to do that very thing. An important client from New York had called earlier asking Mr. Logan to meet him for golf at a nearby resort. He hated to play golf; in fact, he didn't know how to play. But he always made excuses and wouldn't admit the truth. She was convinced that he wanted her to call the client and tell him a lie, and she was just as convinced that she was not going to do it!

She opened the door to his office and peeped in, "Yes?"

"Karen, I need you to call Bill Smith and tell him I can't play golf with him. Tell him my mother is having surgery, and I need to be with her."

"I didn't know she was having surgery."

"She's not. In fact, she's healthier than I am. But he doesn't know that."

"Mr. Logan, I can't tell him something that is not true. I've told you before that it goes against my conscience."

"You're not much help, are you?"

"I guess not. But I do hope you will respect my convictions."

He was obviously irritated. "Just get me the number. I'll call him myself. You act like I'm committing some kind of crime just because I'm telling a little white lie. It doesn't hurt anybody."

∽

Karen is a disciple of Jesus. And because of that, she is committed to having integrity in her life. "Integrity." It is a strong word—one of my favorites. Stephen L. Carter, Yale law professor, tells of a commencement address he once gave. He began his speech by telling the audience he was going to talk about integrity. Mr. Carter describes their response:

The crowd broke into applause. Applause! Just because they had heard the word *integrity*—that's how starved for it they were. They had no idea how I was using the word, or what I was going to say about it, or, indeed, whether I was for it or against it. This celebration of integrity is intriguing: we seem to carry on a passionate love affair with a word that we scarcely pause to define.[1]

Why do so many Americans sing its praises and then 48 percent of us admit to "taking unethical or illegal actions in the past year" on our jobs?[2] What is integrity? How do we, as disciples, define it, and how do we, as working women, practice it?

In his book entitled *Integrity,* Carter distinguishes between "integrity" and "honesty." He says that integrity connotes a consistency of character in choosing right over wrong, whereas honesty is not necessarily noble in its essence. A person can be honest about having done a heinous crime. He can speak clearly about his racist views and be totally honest. But is he having integrity? No, since his basic suppositions about right and wrong are flawed.

As followers of Jesus, we have integrity defined in a person—a person who reflects the very nature of God, who is "the image of the invisible God."[3] Even though their motives were to entrap him, Jesus' enemies spoke truth when they said of him in Matthew 22:16, "Teacher, we know you are a man of integrity and that you teach the way of God in accordance with the truth."

---

[1] Stephen L. Carter, *Integrity* (New York, New York: Basic Books, A Division of Harper Collins Publishers, 1996), 5-6.

[2] "48% of workers admit to unethical or illegal acts," USA Today, 06 April 1997.

[3] Colossians 1:15

Jesus was not only a *man* of integrity, Jesus *was* integrity. Perhaps the best definition of integrity is found in his statement in John:

> "For I have come down from heaven not to do my will, but to do the will of him who sent me.... I do nothing on my own but *speak* just what the Father has taught me. ...for I always *do* what pleases him" (John 6:38, 8:28-29, emphasis added).

As disciples on the job, we must imitate Jesus if we are to have integrity. We need to *speak* and *do* what God has taught us in his Word and what pleases him. In this chapter and the next we will focus on our how our speech and our actions need to reflect the nature of God in our workplaces.

Take a few minutes to read Ephesians 4:25-5:20. This passage sums up the practical workings of "speaking" and "doing" what Jesus taught and what pleases him. I will refer to it in the remainder of this chapter.[4] Our heart should be to "find out what pleases the Lord" (5:10) and to do it!

Integrity of Speech

The words we speak and the way we speak them say much about who we really are. Jesus said,

> "The good man brings good things out of the good stored up in his heart, and the evil man brings evil things out of the evil stored up in his heart. For out of the overflow of his heart his mouth speaks" (Luke 6:45).

---

[4] I would suggest that you do a study of this passage verse by verse at some point, writing down everything it tells you about integrity in the workplace.

No matter how slick and careful we may be, our words will eventually tell the tale on us. They will show us for who we really are—good or bad. They will reveal our hearts.

Jesus spoke just what the Father had taught him; he spoke the very words of God. His heart was one with God, so his words were also.

A philosopher in the first century B.C. said, "Speech is a mirror of the soul: as a man speaks, so is he."[5] All day long people see the reflection of our souls in what we say. As disciples of Jesus in the workplace, what guidelines will help us determine which words will be pleasing to our Lord? The two umbrellas under which we will consider this question are "purity" and "honesty."

Purity of Speech

> But among you there must not be even a hint of sexual immorality, or of any kind of impurity, or of greed, because these are improper for God's holy people. Nor should there be obscenity, foolish talk or coarse joking, which are out of place, but rather thanksgiving (Ephesians 5:3-4).

> "You shall not misuse the name of the LORD your God, for the LORD will not hold anyone guiltless who misuses his name" (Exodus 20:7).

Two pretty clear passages: *No* hint of sexual immorality. *No* obscenity. *No* foolish talk. *No* coarse joking. *No* misuse of God's name. In environments where sexual language is rampant, innuendo is ubiquitous and cursing is the norm, some might wonder,

[5] Publilius Syrus, maxim 1073

What would we talk about? Paul would probably answer that question by saying something else he wrote to the Ephesians, who lived in a pretty depraved environment themselves:[6]

> Do not let any unwholesome talk come out of your mouths, but only what is helpful for building others up according to their needs, that it may benefit those who listen (Ephesians 4:29).

When we are thinking of other people and wanting to meet their needs, then our speech reflects that desire. Our speech reflects the heart of our God.

Your temptation might be (1) to join in such impure conversations because in your old nature you enjoy them, (2) to join in because you do not want others to think you are a prude, (3) not to join in the conversations but to laugh along with others because you are too uncomfortable not to or (4) not to respond in any way (that is, not be willing to say something that could change the environment).

It is important to realize that your sisters all over the world are experiencing the same types of temptations and frustrations that you are. When we are surrounded at work by people who do not have our values and who are not trying to please God with their speech, we can feel alone and sort of "weird." We can imagine that everyone is looking at us as if there were a sign over our heads pointing downward: "This is a really strange person." When you feel your cheeks redden with a flush of embarrassment, just remember your

---

[6] The temple of the "goddess of love" adorned their city along with "priestesses" who were really prostitutes.

connection not only to Jesus, but to your sisters the world over. And don't give in to temptation! Seek to say what pleases the Lord.

Laura, a young married woman, got a job working in a machine shop. She interacted daily with three men: her boss, a salesman and a general manager. Cursing, bad language and sexual comments were frequent and quite offensive to her as a Christian. Should she say something? Was it enough just not to participate in the talk herself?

After praying about it and getting advice, she decided she needed to speak up. God gave her the perfect opportunity: The general manager, while talking with her boss and her, used a swear word. He looked over at her and said, "Excuse me."

Grateful for an inroad, she thanked him for apologizing and told him, "I don't choose to use that language, and it really bothers me to hear it."

His response was quite gracious: "Then we will not do it any more."

She had not self-righteously condemned him. She simply spoke the truth. As a result, the atmosphere is much cleaner than before, and both her boss and her general manager now correct the salesman when he slips.

Two other women shared how they responded to the people who were swearing around them:

> With male coworkers in engineering, swearing is a common practice. Along the way, I had spoken to different engineers, telling them that their swearing bothered me because of my convictions about God. Now it is sort of amusing that whenever we get a new engineer, one of my

Jewish coworkers tells him not to swear around me because of my faith.

-Alice, engineer

Constant cussing from boss and coworkers got to the point that it was making me crazy and angry. I talked to my boss straight on, without sarcasm or condescension, telling him, "It is offensive to me to listen to this language all day. I decided a while ago not to cuss anymore. Could you please try to curb it around me?"

My coworkers kind of kidded me: "Oh, don't cuss around Charlene."

I told them, "Thank you." I appreciated it.

During the farewell lunch at my last job, one of my bosses shared that he actually stopped cussing because of our working together.

-Charlene, marketing associate

Often we find that when we are willing to stand up for our convictions, people respond positively. In fact, they are freed from trying to impress others with inappropriate language. Many people tack it onto and tuck it into their speech just to be accepted. Their consciences are often pricked by someone who has convictions. One sister told me that before becoming a Christian, her language was terrible. But while she was studying, she realized that she needed to change and stopped "cold turkey." People *can* clean up their act more easily than you might imagine. So, if you have never said anything to your coworkers or managers, you may be suffering more than you have to. You won't know their response until you try to communicate your convictions. And if they respond negatively, you can be comforted that you are in good company with Jesus and your working sisters worldwide.

A young man who is an actor recently told me about a situation that is common in his profession. The script for the role he was playing contained some quite offensive lines. He simply changed the words and continued with his lines, a practice which he said usually works fine. But this time someone challenged him to say the words as written. He replied simply, "I don't say those words." At first the rest of the cast thought he was a real prude. But as they got to know him and saw what a great job he did with the role given him, many of the cast members came up to him and told him how much they respected him. Most, if not all, of the cast came with him to church to check out what he was involved in. Had he not taken a stand in maintaining purity of speech, he would never have made such an impact on his peers. The question for us is, "Are we willing to appear 'uncool' in order to express our convictions?"

Another area in which we must pursue purity in our speech is possibly a more challenging one: *gossip.* Solomon understood human nature when he said,

> The words of a gossip are like choice morsels;
>   they go down to a man's inmost parts (Proverbs 18:8).

Naturally speaking, gossip is satisfying. It meets a need in our old natures. It gratifies us as does our favorite food. We savor it. We relish it. Its root is much the same temptation that Satan brought to our mother Eve. It stirs us with a desire to feel powerful, all-knowing, superior, in control—quite appealing to our flesh. And if gossip truly is pleasing "like choice morsels," a feast is served up at the workplace every day. Plates and trays and tables of gossip. Plenty for everyone!

When asked their greatest temptation at work, several women responded as follows, undoubtedly expressing the thoughts of many other women:

> being negative/grumbling and getting drawn into the office gossip.

> frustration and gossip, gossip, gossip!!!! Everybody loves to talk about everybody. I really need to be on top of myself, or I get sucked right into it.

> to gossip and slander people in the office.

> getting into gossip and agreeing with my boss on worldly ideas or worldly discussions because I feel like my boss will not like me if I do not agree or get involved in these discussions.

It is certain that gossip disunifies a group and "separates close friends" (Proverbs 16:28). How do we as disciples handle it when others are gossiping around us or to us?

This was the question a woman named Jill asked herself. She was a tax manager in a big-six firm. After becoming a Christian and cleaning up her act in the swearing area (She says, "I swore all the time"), she faced the decision of how to handle the gossip that swirled around her. She tried several different approaches: (1) bringing up a good point of the person being talked about, (2) simply saying, "This is not productive," and (3) saying, "If you think this is such a problem, why don't you go talk with her about it?" She found that any one of the three tended to take the wind out of the sails of office gossip.

People simply do not enjoy gossiping to someone who does not enjoy listening. As the wise one said,

> Without wood a fire goes out;
>> without gossip a quarrel dies down (Proverbs 26:20).

Don't feed or fan it, and it will die down.

Discernment is needed in defining and avoiding gossip. Not every comment about a person is gossip. There are situations in which we may be asked to give feedback to a manager about someone's performance, and we are not at liberty to talk directly to the person. There are also times when someone honestly needs input as to how to approach a person about an incident or hurt feelings. In this case, we must do everything we can to make sure that the advice-seeker is not just venting on us. We must tell them that they need to talk directly with the person, and we must give good, sound advice about how to do that. If the offended party does not want to take the responsibility to heal the relationship, we should not continue to listen.

Honesty of Speech

> The LORD detests lying lips,
>> but he delights in men who are truthful (Proverbs 12:22).

Therefore, each of you must put off falsehood and speak truth-fully to his neighbor...(Ephesians 4:25).

Some may have seen the movie *Liar, Liar* in which the main character, a lawyer, was wished into a certain situation by his son. It was a very difficult situation indeed: He was unable to lie for twenty-four hours, and he had to speak aloud the truth about every circumstance or person he encountered. To say the very least, his blatant truthfulness cramped his style and got him into a lot of trouble. In the end, though, he learned that telling the truth leaves you feeling more free than ever.

Of course being truthful does not necessarily mean you have to tell someone they have a big nose or a pointed head—even if they do! Tact is not dishonesty, and every truth does not need to be verbalized. We certainly are to "build one another up according to their needs." A big-nosed person is not generally built up by having that truth pointed out to him or her! (It is right before his or her eyes all the time.)

In its many forms and manifestations, lying lurks about us on the job: the boss who tells us to say she is in a meeting, when she clearly stands before us with a pained expression on her face; the coworker who calls in sick, when she obviously feels like going to the beach with her boyfriend; the customer who swears she never wore the shoes outside the house, even though there are deep pits in the soles; and the secretary who is adamant in saying she never received the memo, when it lies concealed in her top drawer.

Why do people lie? To make themselves look better. To make someone else look worse. To get what they want. To further their careers. To protect themselves from ridicule. To seem competent. To keep their jobs...to name a few reasons.

As working women, we have to deal with the temptation to lie on two fronts: (1) *personal lying*—our own decision to lie and (2) *referred lying*—someone else asking us to lie, especially a superior.

Why would we as Christian women be tempted to lie? For all the same reasons that other people are: We want to look better, to make someone else look worse, to get what we want, to further our careers, to protect ourselves from ridicule, to seem competent, to keep our jobs. We know that lying is wrong; that's a given. But it might help us to realize the root motivation that sprouts these aforementioned desires: Stated simply, it is a lack of trust in God or a lack of faith. Lying shows that we do not really believe that he will take care of us if we seek to do his will and to please him. We are saying, in essence, "God I know it would be good to obey you, but you are not strong enough to deal with the consequences of my doing things your way. Therefore, I will give you a break and help you maintain your seeming omnipotence by taking this matter into my own lying hands."

Once and for all we must decide whether we believe in the integrity and power of our God. What does he have to do to prove himself to us? In the words of the old gospel song, "What more can he say / than to you he has said?" We might also add, "What more can he do / than for you he has done?" God promises through

Solomon, "A faithful man will be richly blessed" (Proverbs 28:20). God is faithful to his promises, and he will bless us when we choose to be faithful to him.[7]

Jan was in charge of all accounts receivable at an insurance agency. When I asked her if she had ever been asked to lie by her superiors, she told me the following story:

> All the brokers were to pay their accounts by the end of the year. My managing director was good friends with one of the brokers who wanted to pay after the first of January. My boss wanted me to enter the money as received before January first and to say we had a zero balance (so the office could receive a commission). I refused, saying it was lying. He went ahead and entered the money as received *in my name*. The arrangement was that the broker would give him a kickback.
>
> His boss called me and asked, "Did you receive this money?" I told him the truth. Thankfully he believed me, reprimanded my boss and gave me a $1500 commission for my honesty.

Of course, no one will promise you that your story will always have a happy ending as immediately as Jan's did. For the heroes in chapter 12 of Hebrews, their happy endings did not come until after they died. The following proverb does indicate that our employers will appreciate knowing that since we will not lie *for* them, we probably will not lie *to* them:

> Kings take pleasure in honest lips.
> They value a man who speaks the truth (Proverbs 16:13).

[7] Hebrews 6:18, 10:23; Titus 1:2

As we seek to imitate the integrity of Jesus in our speech at work, may it be said of us as it is said of our God, he "does not lie" (Titus 1:2). Jan does not lie. Charlotte does not lie. Kim does not lie. (Your name) does not lie.

෴

May the work of our hands reward us as we seek to maintain integrity of speech in our workplaces:

> From the fruit of his lips a man is filled with good things
>   as surely as the work of his hands rewards him
>   (Proverbs 12:14).

A Fresh Cup of Life

What does the word *integrity* mean to you?

What is the reputation of your "mouth" at work?

When coworkers use lewd or profane language in your presence, how do you respond? What have been the results of your decisions to speak up or not to speak up?

How do you handle it when someone asks you to lie or to falsify information?

How do you stop the flow of gossip?

In your effort to be righteous, how do you guard against being self-righteous?

What fears do you encounter when you decide to take a stand for integrity?

When we hold back from giving
our best, we are robbing our employers,
and we are robbing God.

CHAPTER 4

❧

Integrity on the Job
Part Two — Integrity of Action

I can see me right now: A little blond, curly-haired girl. (My mother never knew what to do with those curls, so they usually did their own thing). I was in the second grade. Mrs. Killian's room, Alabama Avenue School. In front of me was a small notebook, spiral-bound at the top. Interspersed between the spirals were the faintly printed letters "w-h-i-t-e."

It was time for the weekly spelling test. I was having trouble remembering how to spell "white" and had discovered a foolproof way of getting it right on the test.

I don't think the teacher caught me cheating. Mrs. Killian had a way of turning into a screaming banshee if she got upset with you. So I'm sure I would remember if she found me out.

That was forty-two years ago. I have never forgotten my entry into the world of decision-making and integrity. Thankfully, because of the strong moral teaching and example of my parents, cheating did not become part of my character. As the writer of Proverbs says,

Even a child is known by his actions,
by whether his conduct is pure and right.
(Proverbs 20:11)

❧

What is your reputation at work? If a child is known by his or her actions, then we as adults certainly are too. Do people see you as a hard worker? As a person who gives her best to the team effort? As one who follows through with commitments (or owns up when she doesn't)? As someone who uses her time well and ethically? As a person who can be trusted with company materials and supplies? Although you possibly answered yes to all these questions, is there still room for improvement? Let's take it a little deeper.

Giving Your Best

Slaves, obey your earthly masters in everything; and do it, not only when their eye is on you and to win their favor, but with sincerity of heart and reverence for the Lord. Whatever you do, work at it with all your heart, as working for the Lord, not for men, since you know that you will receive an inheritance from the Lord as a reward. It is the Lord Christ you are serving. Anyone who does wrong will be repaid for his wrong, and there is no favoritism (Colossians 3:22-25).

Though we are not slaves, most of us still answer to someone. The heart attitude of this passage would move us to give our best as if Jesus were our CEO or our immediate supervisor. We should continue day after day to give our best out of respect for him—even if people do not affirm or appreciate us; even if we get into trouble because of our integrity; and even if credit for our ideas is given to someone else or taken by someone else. Our reward is greater than a pay raise, a pat on the back or a promotion.

One woman reported that she was tempted not to give one hundred percent to her job because it is not as important as working for the kingdom. Her comment caused me to remember a time I interviewed for a teaching position. After a very positive and amiable interview, the principal asked a typical ending question, "Is there anything else we should know about you?"

I responded, "Well, I would want you to know that my faith is the most important thing to me and always takes top priority, but because of my faith I will give my very best to this job."

It doesn't matter what we do—sell cars, type reports, clean houses, teach classes, give shots, write books, answer phones, check groceries, conduct hearings, give performances, moderate debates, execute wills, do surgery, etc.—we should give our best. We owe it to our clients/customers, our employers, our employees, our co-workers, ourselves and our God. When we hold back from giving our best, we are robbing our employers, and we are robbing God.

Granted, "giving our best" is a subjective judgment that legalists could painfully stew over and libertines could easily pass over. That is to say, some of us feel guilty when we shouldn't, and others of us don't feel guilty when we should. We simply need to know ourselves and our tendencies, and then we need to ask ourselves how committed we are to do the best we can do without giving our jobs first priority in our lives.

Following Through with Commitments

"Sharon, could you type the notes of the meeting and give them to the others by tomorrow morning?"

"Sure. No problem."

Next morning: "Sharon, got those notes?"

"Uh-h-h, no. Did you ask me to do them? I got back to my desk and couldn't remember who you asked. Then I got busy and forgot to check. If I can remember where I put my handwritten notes, I'll type them up and have them to everyone by the end of the day."

Have you ever done what Sharon did? Has someone ever done to you what Sharon did? If this type of thing is repeated, what happens to the person's reputation for integrity? "Don't ask her; she'll forget. Ask someone more responsible."

Notice that Sharon never took responsibility for her lack of follow-through. She gave excuses. She was slippery. And if no one reprimands her, she will probably do it again and again and try to slide out of it every time. Then what happens when a special invitation women's day comes up in her church? She wants to invite her coworkers, even her boss. She says, "Please come with me to this. I went several years ago, and it truly changed my life." *Yeah, right*, they may think because they do not respect Sharon as a person of her word. Or they may think, *Wow, she must've been even worse back then.*

If you have trouble with follow-through, make a decision to change. You, like me, may not have been "born organized" as some are, and it will take effort for you to change in this area. If you never get deeply convicted to change, you will never change. Get advice from those who are known as people who follow through with whatever commitment they make. Evaluate your responses when people ask you to do something. Do you volunteer without considering whether you can really do it or not? Do you agree simply because you want people to like you or to think that you are a willing worker? Remember the parable about the son who said he would go to work in the vineyard, but then didn't go.[1] He was not pleasing to his father.

Do whatever you need to do in order to remember the commitments you make. Write notes. Use stick 'ems. Put a message on your voice mail. (My husband and I both call our voice-mail boxes at work telling ourselves to do all kinds of things. I even tell myself to have a good morning!) Give responsibility back to others when possible. Sometimes people come up to me at church and ask if I will bring a book to them. My standard reply is, "I would be happy to bring the book, but I'm going to put it on you to call my voice mail and ask me to." That way, the one who has the request on his or her mind is the one who has the greatest responsibility of follow-through. I have tried to learn not to make commitments on the run—they are very easy to forget.

So, take commitments seriously, even seemingly small ones. Never promise anything that you do not build in a reminder to do. When appropriate, put the responsibility back on the one who wants the favor. Be a light that shines to help others know the God

[1] Matthew 21:28-31

who is "faithful to all his promises" (Psalm 145:13) and is not slow in keeping any of them.[2]

Stealing

> He who has been stealing must steal no longer, but must work, doing something useful with his own hands...(Ephesians 4:28).

Since we were kids, most of us heard the ten commandments quoted—especially the eighth one: "You shall not steal" or probably "Thou shalt not steal" (Exodus 20:15). You may have gotten your knuckles hit with a ruler or you may have been sent to the cloakroom (back in the '50s). I remember "swapping" little toys with a younger kid in my neighborhood. I must have manipulated or taken advantage of him in some way because his mother called my mother, and I returned the toys. It is natural for us to see something, to want it and to figure out how to get it. That's exactly what happened in the Garden of Eden.

Many forms of stealing on our jobs beckon us, with more being invented every day. Let's mention a few:

- copying licensed software
- inflating expense reports
- taking office materials
- making long distance calls on the company line

One sister shared her greatest temptation at work: "Software piracy, and picking up small stationery. Often I catch myself and

[2] 2 Peter 3:9

return pens, papers, notepads to my work." We might ask ourselves as Paul asked the Romans, "You who preach against stealing, do you steal?" (Romans 2:21b). We must seek to be employees who live above reproach.

Here again, though, we can get really legalistic. To accidentally take a pen home with you from work and to purposely take home a box of pens are two different things. We should be careful about the former and not make a practice of it, but we should certainly never plan the smuggling of materials. If indeed you have given in to a temptation to outright steal materials, then relent, repent, return and resolve not to do it again.

Consider the heart of the tax collector, Zacchaeus. His profession had a rank reputation: They overcharged their own people, paid the Romans and pocketed the excess. As the passage says, he was a wealthy man. After he came to know Jesus and had him come into his home, his response was to stand up and say,

> "Look, Lord! Here and now I give half of my possessions to the poor, and if I have cheated anybody out of anything, I will pay back four times the amount" (Luke 19:8).

He, no doubt, understood the Old Testament law of retribution:

> "If a man steals an ox or a sheep and slaughters it or sells it, he must pay back five head of cattle for the ox and four sheep for the sheep" (Exodus 22:1).

If those under the old law understood that they must deal radically with stealing, how much more should those of us under the new covenant of grace? Let us make the decision to bend over backwards to avoid even the hint of dishonest behavior. Let us hold up the standard of Christ and not give in to the standard of the world around us:

> Don't let the world around you squeeze you into its own mold, but let God remold your minds from within, so that you may prove in practice that the plan of God for you is good (Romans 12:1-2, J.B. Phillips).

Using Time Well

> Look carefully then how you walk, not as unwise men but as wise, making the most of the time, because the days are evil (Ephesians 5:15-16, NASB).

> Live life, then, with a due sense of responsibility, not as men who do not know the meaning and purpose of life but as those who do. Make the best use of your time, despite all the difficulties of these days (Ephesians 5:15-16, J.B. Phillips).[3]

On the job it takes discernment to "make the best use of your time." We must have a "due sense of responsibility" in order to spend our time wisely. In order to be discerning and responsible, we need to know not only the rules, but the atmosphere of our workplace as well.

When asked, "What are your greatest temptations at work?", several women gave responses that have to do with this area of integrity and time usage:

---

[3] J.B. Phillips, trans. *The New Testament in Modern English* (Indianapolis: The Macmillan Company, 1958).

to goof off (and just look busy), to be late, to abuse my freedom by doing personal stuff on company time or using company materials.

to call or see disciples (there are five of us at my office) and spend too much time talking.

surfing the net and spending too much time on E-mail.

making personal calls or working harder just when my manager looks.

to spend too much time on an unnecessary project.

getting distracted by personal stuff like this [responding to the questionnaire].

to make follow up calls, or call the people in my family group. I have to really watch that, because there are usually many issues that need to be addressed. It is very difficult to leave all these issues until the end of the day, after I get home from work. Plus, since my evenings are usually very busy (my husband and I lead a family group and are the sector administrators), it's very tempting to follow up with nondisciples I'm reaching out to while I'm at work.

taking longer lunches, making personal calls, being late in the morning.

Another woman shared this personal experience:

My conflict actually involves my sin of spending too much time at work doing ministry things. My boss talked to me about this and his reservations about the church. I was so convicted of my unrighteousness. While on the surface it looked like I was serving God, I was actually not bringing glory to him. That boss never had a good impression of the church because of my sin, even though I repented. It is very important to work hard and to do a good job.

Certainly, most employers realize that people need to attend to some personal things from time to time on the job. The day I wrote this chapter I had some insurance situations that I needed to check on, so I needed to call while people were in the billing offices. In the course of our days, all of us will talk on the phone to other disciples or friends or family members. We should take care to limit the length of these calls, though. Except in extremely rare circumstances, deep and involved conversations should be reserved for after-work hours.

To make sure we are maintaining the proper balance on using our time, I asked various people in managerial positions what their expectations were of those who worked under their supervision. Here are some of their responses:

The president of an Internet company with more than 130 employees gave these suggestions:

- Ask for permission in advance; apologies or excuses don't repair integrity damages. If your company doesn't have a policy about private use of the phone, cruising the Internet etc., ask your supervisor for clarification, or don't do it.

- Just because everyone else does it does not mean that it is okay. Managers are no less conflict-avoiders than any one else, i.e. managers often "register" inappropriate behavior without confronting the person.

- Today, more and more companies, particularly in high tech industry, are not interested at all in how much time you are spending at work, but rather what the results of your work are (of course, often eight work hours per day are not enough to meet expectations). Companies with such a culture support the pursuit of private tasks at work. If an employee performs excellently in my company, I don't care about his/her work hours.

Another response came from a Christian who manages approximately thirty people, the majority of which are senior software engineers:

Every manager (who has been a manager very long) understands that people have lots of stuff going on in their lives that cannot always be put on hold while they put in their eight hours. The companies I have worked for have had time-reporting systems that make allowance for non-productive time at work.

I personally believe that the happier people are at work, the more productive they will be for a company. I make sure people know that they have some flexibility on hours, E-mail, Internet, water cooler conferences, and so on.

If people feel respected, they will give their best for you. That's been my experience. It's funny, but so many times people have said things like, "I have a child-care bind tomorrow, and I wanted to know if I could come in late. I'll make it up, of course!" They really want to do the right thing for the most part. So, if you begin with the premise that people want to do the right thing (and believe me, when it comes to protecting a paycheck, they do want to do right!), it has always amazed me how people generally do more for you in the long run, not less.

On the other hand, I've seen managers fail who were too rigid. You try to manage people too tightly and you create bitterness because people, I feel, resent micromanagement.

So, let me summarize. I know people will read and send E-mail, will make phone calls, and will waste some time. I'd rather them do it with my blessing and feel good about my belief in them as individual contributors and see them come through in really important ways rather than me getting my eight hours and not having their loyalty. This *works*! If I see abuses, I address them by asking if there is a problem. (Maybe the guy is on the phone with his lawyer because he is going through a divorce, and here I come and blast away about his hours? Not good. A devastated individual.) But if I see people really getting the job done, working hard, and giving their best, I would like to reward them, not restrict their phone time to get more out of them!

This brother ended his comments with a quip: "Sorry these thoughts are not well organized; after all, I am at work!"

My own manager, who also happens to be my husband, gave me his thoughts on the matter:

It is fine with me for people to have E-mail correspondence and to make some personal phone calls as long as they don't abuse the privilege. In fact, I think it would be very frustrating to have the possibility of communicating with a friend or family member so easily, quickly and inexpensively by E-mail, and then not be able to do it.

(Whew!! No problem with my E-mailing our college daughters!)

The approach of many managers does seem to be, "Relax, but

get your work done!" Others are more rigid in their approach. More strenuous policies may be due to personality and management styles, but they also could be a direct result of the misuse of privileges.

One woman I know works with a government agency in Boston. When I asked for her E-mail address, she hesitated because her management had asked that the employees not use the Internet for personal mail. I was tempted to send her a message and disguise it ("Thursday's meeting"—really a Bible study group), but integrity prevailed. How could I knowingly go against her company's policy and then call her to obey God in our Bible study times together?

Several other people gave helpful responses concerning the use of time at work:

> As a disciple, I strive to make sure that my discretionary time is noticeably less than the average of the people around me.

> Concerning attitude at the work place, I say from experience that management styles have changed incredibly over the years . Though the work ethic is always key, managers realize that good workers are not just those who "plug in their chain" at work, but those who are active in their lifestyles. I work as the information systems coordinator in a human resource department of a major insurance company. I have worked extensively with the new-hire process. We routinely turn down individuals for employment because they show no dynamic interest or ambition in their life. We want to hire people who are movers, and extraordinary people are active in their life-styles.

> In the spirit of not being legalistic, I think that the bottom line is the company should always come out ahead in the

deal, but you don't have to be miserable and/or antisocial in order to make that happen.

Since I am in the role of enforcing my company's electronic media policies, I cannot think of them as foolish or meaningless rules. I am striving to be the example at work in everything that I do. I feel that I must hold to these policies that the company has so that I can be above reproach. For example, we have a policy about no personal Internet E-mail on the company's E-mail system. I had let myself get away with thinking that two or three messages that come a day would be all right. But after asking myself what Jesus' answer would be in this case, I came to the conviction that his response would be completely different. So I set up my own Internet account so that I can continue to receive personal mail. As disciples we need to hold to whatever policies are set before us, no matter what our opinion of them is.

As disciples, we should be working so efficiently and hard that when we take a break to do some nonrelated work the boss is actually happy for us! My boss begged me on numerous occasions to call in sick, even if it was for a so-called "mental-health day."

As a disciple, I try to prioritize, manage my ministry responsibilities like I do my responsibilities at work. What is urgent and important? What can wait until after work? If something cannot wait until after work then I will try to get it done either at lunch or on my breaks.

It is important to know where your company stands on these issues. My company says it is okay to take a minute here and there for a personal call or to pay a bill as long as it doesn't affect what I need to do at work. Since I am paid on salary, I just need to be sure I get everything done that I am supposed to; sometimes I work late and sometimes I am done early.

I feel that disciples have to be careful not to take advantage of Christian employers but rather to do more for the sake of example and integrity. I also think Christians should lighten up on these issues about time usage! If someone has been blowing it by being irresponsible, they should repent and make it their aim to become the very best employee they can be. Then, they will have some flexibility. If they are doing a great job and putting in the extra time when needed and making a valuable contribution, then they need not feel guilty about doing some personal activities on the job.

Remember Paul's injunction to the Ephesians: "Look carefully how you walk, not as unwise men [or women] but as wise, making the most of the time, because the days are evil" (5:15-16, NASB). To sum up this section on integrity in time usage, we could simply say, *Don't be rigid and legalistic, but do obey company policy, and keep personal pursuits to a minimum—to the praise and glory of God.*

Not Always Popular

Integrity. The world loves the sound of it, but very few pay the price to practice it. Be assured that if we diligently practice it, not everyone will be happy about it—especially our coworkers. Why? Because it shows them up. The mirror of our righteousness reflects the flaws of their apathy.

If a per-piece worker puts out too many finished products, the attainable standard becomes obvious. The other workers will say, and usually not very nicely, "Stop working so fast; you're making the rest of us look bad."

If a computer technician asks the boss about certain activities before his conscience frees him to participate, the management might send out an all-department memo forbidding the quietly accepted practice—and this to the consternation of other less conscionable employees. Needless to say, the honest technician will not be nominated for the "Best Buddy of the Month" award by his peers.

If a consultant refuses to record that the recreational meal was work-related, his colleague will plop down his credit card with a huff and a glare.

None of the previous responses is anything new; we can know they are at least 3,000 years old by reading Proverbs:

> Bloodthirsty men hate a man of integrity
> and seek to kill the upright (Proverbs 29:10).

Although, thankfully, most of us do not have contracts put out on our lives for making the decision to be women of integrity at work, people will often be out to "kill" our reputations, to "kill" our chances of advancement, to "kill" our commissions or to "kill" our very employment.

There will also be those who respect us for being true to our convictions. And be assured that they will watch us. One of the "success stories" in the last section of Chapter 5 tells about a woman who was so impressed with the work ethics of her Christian co-worker that she literally invited herself to church with her.

In the work environment it is almost impossible to hide our good works "under a bowl" for very long. Our integrity will be clear for all to see. To some it will be the "smell of death," and they will resent us for it. But for others it will be the "fragrance of life," because it will lead them to the one who himself is integrity.[4]

⌒

If you have worked in children's worship at your church service, you have probably sung the lines, "Be careful little ears what you hear" and "Be careful little mouth what you say" and "Be careful little hands what you do." Interpretation: Have integrity in your speech and in your actions. Each verse ends with the line "For the Father up above is looking down in love." And he is!

> Be careful to do what is right in the eyes of everybody (Romans 12:17).

[4] 2 Corinthians 2:16

A Fresh Cup of Life

Let's take another look at some questions posed at the beginning of the chapter. Give thought and prayer to answering these:

What is your reputation at work?

Do people see you as a hard worker?
…as a person who can be trusted with company materials and supplies?
…as a person who gives her best to the team effort?
…as one who follows through with commitments (or owns up when she doesn't)?
…as someone who uses her time well and ethically?

Although you possibly answered yes to all these questions, how can you still improve in having integrity on your job?

How have coworkers responded to your ethical choices?

What do their responses show you about their hearts?

Sharing your faith at work
can be tricky, confusing, discouraging,
exciting, terrifying and much more.
But one thing it is not, is optional.

CHAPTER 5

God's Ambassador at Work

Sharing Your Faith

Imagine it: You're sitting in your den watching the nightly news. Dinner is in the oven, and you have just stopped for a few minutes to rest. Your feet are propped up on the coffee table, and wouldn't you know it, the phone rings. One of the kids answers and says very loudly (still working on that one), "Mo-o-o-m-m, phone!" You're thinking, *"Mom" just has one syllable; how does he always get two out of it when he calls me to the phone?* Hoping to buy a few more minutes of relaxation, you say, "Is it a solicitor?" To which your son replies, "A what?"

That's it. Got to get up. You answer, "Hello?"

On the other end of the line is a very official-sounding voice saying your name in a very official-sounding way.

"Yes, this is she" (as you try to remember your grammar).

"This is a call from the White House. I will put the President on the line."

Is this a joke? you wonder.

Then you hear the voice. The same voice you just heard on the nightly news. No mistaking it. It is the President. *The* President!

"I was wondering...would consider assuming the office of Ambassador to Bolivia?"

～

Even though very few of us, if any, will ever receive the offer of an ambassadorship from our country, all of us have received an even more important offer:

> We are therefore Christ's ambassadors, as though God were making his appeal through us. We implore you on Christ's behalf: Be reconciled to God (2 Corinthians 5:20).

This is a really big-time ambassadorship—not just between two countries, but between heaven and earth. As God's ambassadors, we have the responsibility of bringing to the world around us his message of reconciliation. Most don't even know that they are at war or that they are in need of reconciliation with God. Enter *Mission: Possible!* We get to tell them with our words, with our commitment, with our lives, with our love.

Specifically, you are God's ambassador at your workplace. Granted, you do not have a special parking place with a neatly lettered sign: Reserved for Ambassador. But you are one all the same.

Sharing your faith at work is multifaceted. It can be tricky, confusing, discouraging, exciting, terrifying and much more. But one thing it is not, is optional. Before ascending to his Father in heaven, Jesus was very clear about the mission he was placing into the hands of the disciples and into the hands of those the disciples would bring to him throughout the ages: you and me, specifically. No sealed envelope with an encoded message. No cassette tape that would self-destruct in five minutes. Just the word of the Son of God and no chance of misunderstanding:

> Then Jesus came to them and said, "All authority in heaven and on earth has been given to me. Therefore go and make disciples of all nations, baptizing them in the name of the Father and of the Son and of the Holy Spirit, and teaching them to obey everything I have commanded you. And surely I am with you always, to the very end of the age" (Matthew 28:18-20).

As clear as the mission was the promise: "I am with you always, to the very end of the age." Well, guess what: The age isn't yet over. Granted, it is a long age, but it will not be over until Jesus returns in the same way that he left.

As you walk into work every day, remember Jesus saying, "I am with you always." That means "I am with you now!" "You are not alone." "You are my specially chosen ambassador; together we will get the job done."

Being Real

Sharing our faith does not always mean verbally telling someone about Jesus or the church. Our daily lives—actions, reactions, interactions—share much about who we are and who we imitate. The Word "becomes flesh" once again as we live it. The fruit of the

Spirit in our lives produces the seeds for others to know God. (See Chapter 7.) In order for people to desire our way of life, we must come across as real people, not plastic or stained-glass versions of personhood. Sometimes we are so aware of needing to be good examples that we freeze up and become rigid. We are afraid of admitting when we make mistakes or when we respond unkindly in a situation. The truth is that people who work with us day in and day out will see us sin. Accept it. Then deal with it in a righteous way that will help them to learn how they should be dealing with sin too. We must learn to relax and to be friends to people. We cannot right every wrong they do or say. We cannot wait until someone totally cleans up his or her act and becomes a disciple before we affirm the good things we see in their lives. Friends convert friends. That is healthy, but it is not necessarily easy for most of us.

Because of the gossip, bad language, dirty jokes and complaining attitudes of those around us, we want to withdraw. What a tightrope we sometimes seem to walk! As disciples we must be discerning and learn to balance the following two scriptures:

> I have written you in my letter not to associate with sexually immoral people—*not at all meaning the people of this world* who are immoral, or the greedy and swindlers, or idolaters. In that case you would have to leave this world (1 Corinthians 5:9-10, emphasis added).

> But among you there must not be even a hint of sexual immorality, or of any kind of impurity, or of greed, because these are improper for God's holy people. Nor should there be obscenity, foolish talk or coarse joking, which are out of place, but rather thanksgiving. For of this you can be sure: No immoral, impure or

greedy person—such a man is an idolater—has any inheritance in the kingdom of Christ and of God. Let no one deceive you with empty words, for because of such things God's wrath comes on those who are disobedient. *Therefore do not be partners with them* (Ephesians 5:3-7, emphasis added).

Paul says that we obviously need to "associate with" people who are worldly, but we should not become "partners with" them. We are not to purposely place ourselves with people who corrupt our hearts and minds. If this is happening at work and we have already spoken up, we will need to make wise choices. We may no longer be able to sit with certain people at lunch because they persist in improper talk, but we can still seek to be their friends. Learning to *engage* but not to *indulge* is the goal, to "associate with" but not to be "partners with."

Jesus certainly had in mind mixing it up with people to affect their lives when he gave the following comparison:

He told them still another parable: "The kingdom of heaven is like yeast that a woman took and mixed into a large amount of flour until it worked all through the dough" (Matthew 13:33).

We may feel like a very small packet of yeast as we look at the huge lump of dough that is our workplace, but Jesus reminds us of the power of that yeast. We must be real with people, become friends with them and share our own lives with them before their spirits "rise" to want to know God.

Patti, a chemist at a research university, shares about becoming friends with a coworker:

I had a woman work with me as a temporary worker. She and I developed a great friendship and were able to talk about many spiritual things as we worked. I was able to encourage her to pursue a job in her major. While she came to Women's Day and started to study the Bible, she did not pursue it. She is in a different city today, and I still pray that she will become a Christian. Her friendship was very special to me and allowed me to see God working through me in the workplace.

Being real also means letting someone know if we are upset with them or if they have hurt us. During a short stint of teaching social studies in middle school, I dealt with frustration over the use of a VCR. It had been bought *for* the social studies department *by* the social studies department. The idea was that I would have a VCR to use whenever I needed it. I came in one day, planning to use it for all five periods, and it was gone. I searched and found it in the room of one of the science teachers. A seasoned teacher in the school told me to take it back to my room and leave a note to the science teacher that she would need to get one from the library. So I did.

Then several days or so later, the same science teacher sent two students one at a time to ask if she could borrow the VCR. Each time I said, "No, I am going to be using it." The interruptions broke the concentration of the already easily distracted class, and I was really put out with this teacher.

I knew I needed to talk with her, but I did not want to. (Not many of us love a situation that involves potential conflict.) When we did talk, I was honest but kind, telling her exactly what was bothering me. I also let her know that I wanted us to have an amiable relationship and did not want there to be any tension between us.

In a subsequent interview with the superintendent of education, he asked what I could particularly bring to the school setting that would be unique and helpful. I recounted this instance to him. I said that judging from the talk in the teachers' lounge, many people do not resolve their differences; they just talk behind each other's backs.

We would like to think that as disciples we are above getting upset with others, but we are not. God calls us to be real, to repent when needed, to resolve differences with others, and "as far as it depends on [us]," to "live at peace with everyone" (Romans 12:18).

Listening and Caring

We've probably all heard the old adage, "People don't care how much you know until they know how much you care." How true it is. The wise one said, "A kindhearted woman gains respect..." (Proverbs 11:16). People can tell whether we really care about them or are just doing the right thing in a perfunctory way. We can ask someone to come to church or to study the Bible and feel justified in our hearts, "Well, I asked her; she's just not open." But, did we care about her and find ways to show her that we cared?

Lara is a twenty-six-year-old single woman who manages the business development of her company on the West Coast. She shared her experience in reaching out and becoming a friend to a coworker:

Last October my discipler pointed out that I was not really giving my heart to anyone in the world. I had gotten to a place where I was really guarded because I had brought so many people to church who had either not become disciples or who became disciples and then fell away. I felt like a failure and did not want to go through it again (selfish, selfish, selfish).

So after her challenge, I got a bunch of goodies and made cards and gave various women in my office Halloween gifts. Three of those women started warming up to me after that. One of them started going to the movies with me every Friday. She has slowly gotten to know more and more disciples. She has been able to be really open with them. (Though the idea of God and church was like a trip to Mars for her.)

She came to Women's Day, and last Sunday she finally made it to church! And when I walked her to church, she said she was definitely coming again next week! She also agreed to study, but she is feeling a little unsure because she has absolutely no religious background. After Women's Day she told me her life story. One of the things that really convicted me was she said she had been really suicidal for most of last year. You would never have guessed this if you met her. She said that those urges left her late last October. On my way home that night I realized that was when I gave her that Halloween candy!

The greatest way to show caring is probably the simple act of listening. In our fast-paced society, people have little time to talk and no time to listen. When you give people focused attention and ask questions about their families and their lives, they generally appreciate it. They may at first wonder, *What's in it for her?* But genuine love casts out the skepticism.

Taking Advantage of Opportunities

Devote yourselves to prayer, being watchful and thankful. And pray for us, too, that God may open a door for our message, so that we may proclaim the mystery of Christ, for which I am in chains. Pray that I may proclaim it clearly, as I should. Be wise in the way you act toward outsiders; *make the most of every opportunity*. Let your conversation be always full of grace, seasoned with salt, so that you may know how to answer everyone (Colossians 4:2-6, emphasis added).

Since we are paid to work for our school, hospital, store, studio or company, and not paid to share our faith, we must be responsible and discerning on the job. We cannot spend long periods of time studying or talking about the Bible with others. But, God does give us opportunities here and there to share. We must have keen spiritual eyes and open, receptive hearts so the Spirit can move us, as he did Philip, to take advantage of an opportunity for the sake of the kingdom:

Then Philip ran up to the chariot and heard the man reading Isaiah the prophet. "Do you understand what you are reading?" Philip asked.

"How can I," he said "unless someone explains it to me?" So he invited Philip to come up and sit with him (Acts 8:30-31).

When people "invite" us into their lives audibly or simply by showing need, we must be ready with conversation that is "always full of grace, seasoned with salt, so that [we] may know how to answer everyone." Just as children have specific and rare moments of teachability, so do adults. Our daily walk with God should be others-focused enough to recognize these moments.

Here are some comments from disciples who recognized teachable moments and initiated "Colossians 4" conversation:

My previous supervisor has gone thorough a tough time in her marriage and life in general. I had many opportunities to share my life with her, and she has consistently wanted to know more. She seems to call me when she needs help, and although she is not, as she puts it, ready to try church, she welcomes the input and direction. I respect her very much, and it took a long time for me to believe that I had something to give to her—something that she needs.

-Elaine, human resources supervisor

There was a time when my director was really struggling with being known as the "Witch of the West." She caused a lot of division and low morale in our department. There were days when she would leave work crying because she didn't know how to handle it. She didn't want to be like that. Anyway, the VP called a meeting with us about restructuring our department, and he revealed her real feelings to us. I think I was the only one in that room who had compassion on her because I was struggling with the same thing at the same time!

The next day I went into my director's office, told her what was said at the meeting and that I could totally relate to her. I understood what she was going through because I have had the same struggles. I also told her that if she needed anyone to talk to, I would be there. She was amazed. She asked me how I am always so calm and happy. I ended up telling her that it was because of God. "I couldn't do this on my own." I told her that I went to a great church, and she said that it was funny that I mentioned church, because someone told her that she should start going to church. I shared my life briefly, and she was really impacted. She ended up telling her assistant that I totally made her day. Wow! Me, a lowly "assistant," sharing with a director! That was the boldest sharing I've ever done at work.

-Tracy, production assistant

I recently asked one of the women to come to a Bible study with me and she was very receptive. I tried to be wise about when/how I talked to her and waited until some of the others were gone. I really want to build strong relationships at work and give each individual a chance to hear the gospel. I used to do it in a group setting and found the individual approach is much more effective.

-Deb, medical transcriptionist

Being Patient

I had lunch with my friend Debby yesterday. She is married and has two children. She is also vice president in charge of community development in a large bank. As we talked about bearing fruit at work, her comment was, "Be patient. Take time to build." She said at one point she would invite people quickly to church or to a Bible study. Not many responded by actually coming. But as she persevered in living the life at work, people were affected.

One woman began to study the Bible and gave as her reason for doing so: "When we were working together, you would never talk about other people. That made me know that I could trust you." She did not become a Christian, but she did have the opportunity to hear God's message because Debby shared *and* lived her faith on the job.

As she continued to build, day after day, she introduced a man to her husband, Stan. Before long the man was studying the Bible, and Stan was able to baptize him into Jesus.

When you work with people daily, you must do more than just ask them to church. You must be patient and give the harvest time to ripen. Give to people, and look for those opportunities from God to share with them. Jesus told us to "open [our] eyes and look at the fields! They are ripe for harvest." He wants workers in the field. Will you be his worker in your field?

Being Bold

Amen for being patient, but patience should never be an excuse for not being bold. Patience does not negate boldness. Patience has to do with trusting God for right timing. Boldness has to do with trusting God and saying what needs to be said or doing what needs to be done, no matter what the consequences. In our natures we tend one way or the other: toward patience or toward boldness. Or could it be more accurately stated: toward cowardice or toward insensitivity? The cross always calls us to the center of God's will: neither to the right nor to the left.

Most of us do not want to rock the boat in our work situations. We are simply afraid that if we do, we will fall out (or be thrown overboard). I can remember sitting at the table in the teachers' lounge and wondering when or if I should say something. Although I knew all the teachers pretty well, I was actually a "substitute"— not really one of them. Was it really my place to speak up when I felt they were being unprofessional and maybe even cruel in the way they talked about a student? At that point I decided just to be a positive example. But since then I have felt that I should have said something—not to the whole group at once, but privately to the individuals I knew personally.

In another situation I was working with two teachers and a parent to put on a middle-school talent show. We had fewer students try out for the show than we had anticipated. So the kids were asking one of the teachers, "Is everybody who is trying out going to be in the show?" Since she thought they would not feel as special if everyone was going to be in it, she wanted to lie and say, "No. Everyone will not be in it."

I said, "But that's lying. There is a way to respond that is not lying. You can say, 'Those of us on the committee are the only ones who need to know how many are chosen.'"

She said, "Yeah. That's good."

Since it was natural for her to lie in such a situation, she simply did not think about how she could respond in a truthful way.

Boldness in expressing our convictions about God, Jesus, the Bible or our church is imperative. How often, though, have we been like Peter? In the inspiration of the moment with Jesus he said, "Even if I have to die with you, I will never disown you" (Matthew 26:35). Then that very night he swore, "I don't know the man!" (26:74).

During our prayer times in the morning, or when we are together with our Christian sisters, we, like Peter, say to Jesus, "Even if I have to die with you, I will never disown you." Then, in the press of the day and the embarrassment of the moment, we shrink back as if to say, "I don't know the man!" Sometimes Jesus just doesn't seem to fit in our workplaces. In fact, that is why he was crucified: He just didn't seem to fit. Are we ashamed of him? Are we too cool to be associated with him? Too afraid to be thought of as strange or as a goody-two-shoes?

Lord, we believe. Help our unbelief!

Success Stories

It always encourages us to hear success stories. They inspire us. They call us to hang in there. They buoy our sinking faith. Here are a few:

> I was met by a sister named Linda whom I worked with thirteen years ago. I had just started a new job, and I was impressed by Linda's work ethics. She was always working, even during the down times when there seemed to be nothing to do. She trained me for my job and one day happened to start talking about what she was learning from a Bible study group that she was attending. She never actually invited me to church or Bible study; I invited myself because of the respect I had for her by watching her at work. After two months of studying the Bible, I became a disciple.
>
> *-Andrea*

> I was working for a major community mental health center in Washington state. I would always stop and talk with Claudette, a very spiritual person who was in charge of the records room. I was, at the time, an associate minister in a church.
>
> She eventually invited me to have dinner with her and her husband, a minister himself. I went with a lot of arrogance and figured I could teach her husband some things.

Well, he began to explain the church to me, and we read lots of Scripture that night. After I left, I was convinced that this was the church I had been looking for all of my life. I was baptized about one month later.

-*Hardy*

A woman named Holly got a page from her boss, and my office "just happened" to be the nearest one, so she came in and asked if she could use my phone. I was searching for God at that point, and my desktop was covered with religious books of all sorts. She noticed them and said, "Oh, I see that you are religious." I went to a group Bible study a couple of weeks later and was baptized about a month later. I was forty-five years old, and she was barely twenty.

-*Don*

I am a single mom and was reached out to by a fellow nurse while working at a hospital. She was actually receiving a lot of persecution from the other nurses, and I felt compassion for her! She saw my heart, I guess, because she persevered with me, building a friendship, and inviting, inviting, inviting, until I finally attended a service after eighteen months.

-*Janet*

I was met by a woman named Karin who was a waitress. Before I found out she was a Christian, I had an interest in her. She was always nice and easy to talk to. She had a way of putting others before herself, and it was a genuine action—I mean it wasn't a cover-up. Karin was sharing with another man about the church. I had overheard the conversation and felt a strong urge to ask her about the church. When I did, she told me it was a young church. I can't remember the whole conversation, but she did invite me to the service that Sunday. I was a little weirded out by how it happened, but I went to the service. The sermon was just what I need to hear. It fit my life and spoke to where I was at that moment. Amen! She is now my spiritual "mom."

-Tim

A man named Gordon worked at the management and sales training company in Boston where I worked. My perception of him was not kind—I thought of him as a "Bible-banger." I was on an activity planning committee for the company at the time, and he came before our committee to propose the idea of a group Bible study at the company. After he left the room, we all laughed and said, "If we let Gordon start his Bible study group, we'll have to let the Moonies start one too."

I was searching for God at the time, but in all the wrong places. I thought psychology had answers and tried different religions, including transcendental meditation. I thought the Bible was a book written by man. Of course, I had read little of it.

I went to Toronto the following year to help open an office and returned to Boston in a much more humble state. God moved a disciple into my building, which I didn't realize until later. He also had a sister named Becca, whom Gordon knew, interview at the company. I thought she was much too nice and probably couldn't handle the job. She did get the job, however. I knew she called herself a Christian, and I watched her closely. She invited all the people in the department to a "Bring Your Neighbor Day." (She later told me that of all the people she had invited, she thought I was the least likely to go.)

I was willing to try anything once. I also thought I might find someone to date there. But God had prepared my heart for much greater things. I was totally amazed at what I found and heard when I went to the service. What I heard from God's word rang true. It made total sense and touched me deeply. I asked Becca, "Where do I start?"

She gave me her Bible. I went home and started reading and have not put it down since. I was baptized fifteen
years ago. I am so thankful for God, for Gordon and for
Becca, who was willing to reach out to me at work.

-another Janet

None of the Christians in the previous examples knew how
the seeds they were planting would grow. They were simply being
faithful to sow. God gave the increase when the seeds fell into good
soil. These women probably do not feel like heroes. Each one of
them has her good days and her bad days, her victories and her
defeats, her strengths and her inadequacies. They, like each of us,
are simply people who looked for opportunities and did their best
to share what they had found. God did the rest.

⁓

Be faithful. Sprinkle spiritual salt in your workplace, and be
ready to share the living water when people become aware of
their spiritual thirst:

"...whoever drinks the water I give him will never thirst. Indeed,
the water I give him will become in him a spring of water welling
up to eternal life" (John 4:14).

A Fresh Cup of Life

What does it mean to you that you are God's ambassador at your workplace?

List several adjectives describing how you feel about sharing your faith with people at your workplace.

How relatable are you to people at work?

What can you do to be more relatable without compromising any convictions?

Would you say that you are on the lookout for opportunities to share with people throughout the day?

In what ways do you struggle with being patient? With being bold?

What specific commitment will you make in order to be more effective in your outreach at work?

The difference between
the sexes introduces inherent power and
possible problems in any societal arena —
especially the workplace.

CHAPTER 6

ᛒ

Warm but Wise

Relationships with Male Coworkers

"May I come in for a moment?"

Sonya looked up from her stack of invoices. Marty from the sales office stood at the door.

"Sure. Have a seat."

He closed the door behind him and sat down. His nervousness evaporated as he looked her straight in the eyes. "You are the most beautiful woman I have ever seen or known. I am convinced that God means for us to get to know each other. Is there any chance of that happening on your part?"

After he finished, a look of embarrassment replaced the focused boldness. Neither of them knew what to say.

She regained her composure and said with a calm, though quivering voice, "In the first place, I am not comfortable with your coming in my office and closing the door behind you. I prefer to have all my conversations with men in full, public view. And in the second place, it is inappropriate for you to express your thoughts to me like this. I want to make it clear to you that I am first and foremost a follower of Jesus, and I date only men who share this commitment with me. And, in fact, I do already have a boyfriend."

"I am so sorry. I can't believe I actually came in here and said what I did."

Marty stood up and made a hasty retreat, not even daring to look back. He shut the door quietly behind him.

Sonya was left alone with her thoughts: *Did I do anything to encourage his interest? I certainly have noticed that he is nice-looking. Should I have reacted more than I did? Was that a line, or was he sincere about his desire to be with me? How do I act the next time I see him? Will my boyfriend understand? What counsel will my discipler give me? Should I mention something to my manager?*

❧

Male and female relationships have confused many issues through the years…starting way back in the Garden of Eden. We understand that males and females are to date and fall in love and get married and have children. But can they be friends? Can they be coworkers? Can they have relationships that do not lead to dating, falling in love, marrying and having children? Let's hope so, or things are going to be really confusing in the work world!

In the church, relationships between men and women can be rewarding, encouraging, pure and inspiring. God made us with this potential in our relationships. I'm thankful for the men who are in the lives of my husband and me. But I also have great respect for the difference between my relationships with my brothers in Christ and with my sisters. Though I feel close to my brothers, there are liberties I will not take with them. Wisdom teaches me to be careful, and I try really hard to listen to her. Because Satan loves to catch us unawares, how important it is for us as Christian women to be wise and careful in our relationships with male coworkers.

One of the main concerns for a Christian in the workplace is to have relationships that are characterized by purity. The book of Proverbs tells us

> The LORD detests the thoughts of the wicked,
>   but those of the pure are pleasing to him (Proverbs 15:26).

Paul says we are to conduct our lives without "even a hint of sexual immorality, or of any kind of impurity…because these are improper for God's holy people" (Ephesians 5:3). To be holy is to be set apart, to be different. At the office, hospital, school or store, we should be set apart from others in our pursuit of purity. I say "pursuit" of purity because we must set our minds to go after it. Do not think that it will come to us naturally. That's why Paul told Timothy to flee ungodly desires and to pursue godly qualities:

> Flee the evil desires of youth, and pursue righteousness, faith, love and peace, along with those who call on the Lord out of a pure heart (2 Timothy 2:22).

As women we must do our part to discourage men from thinking impurely about us or being drawn to us sexually. But, no matter how careful we are in our dressing and our actions, worldly men will sometimes make comments (and passes). Thankfully, though, because of the tougher standards about sexual harassment nowadays, men tend to be much more self-controlled in their responses to women.

We can be grateful for less-overt statements and actions on the part of men, but we must also be on guard against the smooth operators who view stronger sexual harassment guidelines as a challenge to their craft. They know not to make lewd or suggestive comments or to sexually touch their female coworkers, but they can get their messages across in a more subtle manner. They can "worm their way" into the hearts of women by being considerate and complimentary: "Hey, I like your new haircut!" or "Nice dress," or "Does your husband know how lucky he is?"[1] They can also be very empathetic listeners (although their wives may not see that side of them very often).

A married disciple with a responsible position in a firm told me about an encounter she had with a man right before I interviewed her for this book. He said to her, "I feel almost silly saying this, but I'm very attracted to you."

The sister responded in an extremely firm tone, "What do you mean by that? If it is anything other than the context of what we are doing, then you are very out of line here. I am a happily married woman. I have no interest in you in that way, and you need to know that." Her body language emphasized every word she spoke.

[1] 2 Timothy 3:16

He quickly responded with, "I'm sorry if I offended you," and that was the last she has heard from him on that topic. They have continued to work on a project together, but he clearly understands her stance and her convictions.

A man can seem humble and apologetic after sharing in such a way, but we must not forget that the sharing was inappropriate. We must not be too eager to make him feel at ease. We should never excuse his actions or we could be opening the door to new tactics in the future. His seemingly awkward admission could have been a politically correct way to "test the waters" and make it easy for either a hasty retreat or an inappropriate step toward emotional attachment.

We must also realize that some men are not purposefully manipulative; they are simply lonely. They don't know how to connect with women emotionally. They may not even be aware of why they feel drawn to Christian women—partially because we are helpful and kind to people, men included. Since we are accustomed to interacting with our brothers, we can be naive as to the ultimate intentions of most men who are not disciples. Coworkers can misconstrue our responses to them. One woman pointed out that worldly men can easily misinterpret our friendliness. In fact, they could even view it as flirting. In the words of Jesus, we must be "as shrewd as snakes and as innocent as doves" (Matthew 10:16b).

Be on guard if men share their feelings for you. Also beware if they share their personal hurts or fears or disappointments. Whether they are being sincere or manipulative, either way it is emotionally entrapping. Require absolute professionalism (not a spiritual term, but one that communicates with men in your workplace). And know that you are totally within your bounds to tell them very clearly what your convictions are. Do not allow them to confuse your kindness and biblical humility with weakness and take-advantage-of-me vulnerability. The "Proverbs 31 woman" is described as being "clothed with strength and dignity" (v. 25). That's a good way to think of yourself at your workplace. Each day as you "clothe [yourself] with compassion, kindness, humility, gentleness and patience," remember to add "strength and dignity" to your spiritual outfit.

Guidelines

In preparing to write this chapter I asked many women to respond to the following question: "What guidelines do you use to determine the way you interact with male coworkers?" Let me share with you some of their insightful responses:

> Usually, I make sure that other female coworkers are with me and the male. I share my faith with them, but not in a preachy kind of way; it is more a sharing of my life (with caution). I try to get them to come to church if possible so that they can meet and build relationships with brothers. I also try to stay in a very public area in the office or when I need to have lunch meetings, etc...
>
> *-Artonya, single, technical recruiter*

> I let them know up front that I am happily married, and that I don't appreciate "off-color" jokes, and that I am a Christian.
>
> *-Joy, married, project manager/software engineer*

In regard to daily contact and work: I try to focus on being humble and real and always address issues that make me feel uncomfortable with honesty and straightforwardness. I do not tolerate any "hints" that are ungodly whatsoever, but it is extremely vital to be humble and quick to resolve it. No one-on-one meetings to discuss past moments of "inappropriateness." I try not to make it a big deal...just address it when it happens. If it happens in a group, I ask the man to stay afterwards for a second and lay out firmly, but respectfully, my boundaries.

It's incredibly important to pray a lot when Satan starts this tactic. Pray for wisdom and do not give in to fear and be "reactionary." These men need to see Jesus, but a clear line needs to be drawn as well to help them see your life and doctrine matching up.

-Gina, single, corporate events specialist

For the most part, this has not been a problem in my workplace. I find that inviting a person who is interested in more than friendship to church or Bible study usually quenches the impure inclinations in conversation.

-Sylvia, single, research associate

Stay on a business-related subject. If anything personal comes up I always bring up God, my church, Jesus, etc.

-Ann, single mom, software engineer

When I am tempted to lust, I look the other way. I also avoid one-on-one situations with any male coworker (like meetings and lunches).

-"Sarah," married, project manager

I make sure that my male coworkers are aware that I am happily married to a wonderful man. I let them know that I want them to meet him. I talk to them about my marriage relationship, stating that although there are bumps, we always resolve them.

-Judy, married, sales assistant

Looking back over the preceding statements, I drew up the following list of suggestions for relationships with men at work:

- Avoid being alone with male coworkers.
- Have one-on-one meetings in a public place or with the door/window blinds open.
- Let them know that you are a Christian.
- Share your faith without getting too personal.
- Find a way for them to build relationships with brothers.
- If you have a boyfriend, let them know and talk about him.
- If you are married, let them know your commitment to your husband (and children).
- When tempted to lust, look the other way.
- Be real and humble, but professional.
- One extra: Talk to them about their families.

If something inappropriate does come up:

- Do not tolerate hints of impurity.
- Be firm, but not unkind or over-reactive, in setting someone straight.
- State clearly what offends you about their behavior.

Working on this book and hearing from so many women has caused me to be proud of my sisters around the world who are following Jesus as they go to work every day or every night (depending on their shift!). They care about the men with whom they work, but realize how important it is to have specific guidelines in their interactions with them; thus, they are not as easily caught off guard if someone does act in an inappropriate way toward them. If you have not thought through your own personal guidelines for your interactions with men in your workplace, take a minute to do so. Jot down any others that you thought of that are not on the previous list.

Be Wise and Beware

One last caution in this area: I heard from one disciple who has been in the work world for many years. She had been the recipient of several overt forms of sexual harassment through the years, but had been repelled by each. *This is not a problem area for me*, she thought. *I love my husband and children; I would never commit adultery.* But later she was caught off guard. She found herself thinking and talking a great deal about the man for whom she worked. They had much in common, and he expressed genuine appreciation for her talents and strengths. He was frustrated in his marriage, and her marriage, though to a disciple, was not emotionally fulfilling. Slowly, but surely, she was falling in love with this man who so freely shared his thoughts and feelings with her.

Thankfully, she awoke to what was happening emotionally, and distanced and disentangled herself before she crashed spiritually, possibly taking her husband and children over the cliff with her.

Now she is very careful in work situations. She no longer tells herself, *This could never happen to me.* Now she heeds Paul's warning in 1 Corinthians 10:12: "So, if you think you are standing firm, be careful that you don't fall." When she moves to a new workplace, she quickly identifies any man she is drawn to (there is something to this chemistry thing!). She then tells her discipleship partner or a close sister who he is, and she avoids personal contact with him as much as possible. She is wise, and we would all be wise to learn from her. Married women, don't forget that you are human. Establish guidelines and stick to them, even if you think you don't need them.

Singles, don't forget that you are human too. Satan would love to dangle a sensitive, nice-looking, attentive man in front of you (especially if none of the brothers are initiating time with you). A single woman told me about her temptation as worldly men began to give her praise and attention in the wake of several rejections by Christian men. She caught herself and realized that since she had a relationship with Jesus, she had more than any non-Christian had—married or single. Many single women who fall away from their faith are ones who compromise for the love of a non-Christian man. Sisters, nothing is worth your relationship with God. Don't ever pay such a tragically high price in order to cuddle up to warm flesh.

Simply establishing and sticking to guidelines is not enough. For the best protection spiritually, be open on a temptation and thought level. Don't be like the Pharisees. They looked good on the outside but were full of sin on the inside. Let your sisters help you guard your heart.

A Godly Response

Not every woman has had to deal with inappropriate advances in the workplace. Several women responded along the lines of the following:

I'm really grateful for my work environment. All my male coworkers are married and some have children. I haven't received any sexual harassment, flirting or sexual innuendoes in almost two years of working here. My boss is very family oriented and he's been to our church before with his wife, so I feel comfortable talking to him. However, most of the time I try and keep our relationship on a professional level while at work.

-Nanette, single, executive assistant

My current manager is a man, and we have a very professional relationship. He is married and has kids, and he respects my devotion to my family. He has never made any advances in any way.

-Joy, married, project manager/software engineer

How should we respond if a male coworker is inappropriate? Again, let's hear from other women who are on the front lines of the battle.

When the flirting comes up, I share my faith with the man and give him brothers' phone numbers. Now that I am dating, I let him know that I have a boyfriend and tell him that I do not appreciate the flirting. When I have felt attracted to a coworker, I pray about my heart and my purity and ask God to take the lust away.

-Artonya, single, technical recruiter

Strictly business at all times, and if there is a hint of inappropriateness, I change the subject. If it continues, I ask the person to stop the behavior and explain my convictions about purity or righteousness and slip in an invitation to church. An idea: Invite brothers to visit you at work and introduce them to the coworker.

-Gina, single, corporate events specialist

I haven't received any sexual harassment that couldn't be stopped with a "cut-it-out" look, but I have on occasion been flirted with and had unwanted sexual innuendo focused at me. I usually make sure I pointedly ignore it... i.e. if some guy comes up and tries to rub my back while I am talking to him, I make sure I move out of the way, remove his hands gently but firmly, and keep talking about work. Other times (depending on what is said) I will simply and immediately turn my back and walk away. Doing this usually gets me an apology from the offender for his actions."

-Joy, married, project manager/software engineer

I have been sexually harassed at least twice. I first told each of them to stop what he was doing (holding my wrist, touching my shoulders, etc.). At times they wouldn't stop. I even had to hit someone so they would let go of me (this was before I was a disciple). After that, I reported it to my supervisor, who in turn told me to write a letter to the corporate office. It definitely stopped after that.

The men that I work with now tend to stay strictly on professional terms. However, I do have those one or two men who tend to make flirtatious comments. In that case, I make sure that I set them straight and tell my husband and discipler. By doing that, I keep my heart open and pure.

-Tracy, married, production assistant

With the current rise in sexual harassment suits, all I have to do is say, "What you just did can be considered sexual harassment." With this statement, they tend to back off.

-Judy, married, sales assistant

Sexual Harassment

Our brother Paul set us an example of using the law to protect us when possible. He and Silas were severely flogged and thrown into prison with their feet in stocks (Acts 16:23-34). When they were told the next day that they could go free, Paul said to the officers, "They beat us publicly without a trial, even though we are Roman citizens, and threw us into prison. And now do they want to get rid of us quietly? No! Let them come themselves and escort us out" (Acts 16:37).

The US and other countries have very clear laws concerning sexual harassment. If anyone violates the law toward you, tell the appropriate authorities. To be able to identify sexual harassment, read the following excerpt of material published by the EEOC (Equal Employment Opportunities Commission) of the United States Government:

> Sexual harassment is a form of sex discrimination that violates Title VII of the Civil Rights Act of 1964. Unwelcome sexual advances, requests for sexual favors, and other verbal or physical conduct of a sexual nature constitutes sexual harassment when submission to or rejection of this conduct explicitly or implicitly affects an individual's employment, unreasonably interferes with an individual's work performance or creates an intimidating, hostile or offensive work environment.
>
> Sexual harassment can occur in a variety of circumstances, including but not limited to the following: The victim as well as the harasser may be a woman or a man. The victim does not have to be of the opposite sex. The harasser can be the victim's supervisor, an agent of the employer, a supervisor in another area, a coworker, or a non-employee. The victim does not have to be the person harassed but could be anyone affected by the offensive conduct. Unlawful sexual harassment may occur without economic injury to or discharge of the victim. The harasser's

conduct must be unwelcome. It is helpful for the victim to directly inform the harasser that the conduct is unwelcome and must stop. The victim should use any employer complaint mechanism or grievance system available.[2]

Notice the statement: "It is helpful for the victim to directly inform the harasser that the conduct is unwelcome and must stop." This should give you even more confidence in saying to someone, "I find your conduct offensive, and I am asking you to stop."

And note one other thing: The harassment can be from male to female, from female to male, from female to female and from male to male. A woman from the West Coast wrote that she has had to deal with sexual innuendoes, jokes and passes from lesbians. Disciples who are from this type of background (as well as those who are not) can be tempted in this area. This sister was as firm in her communication with the offending women as she would have been with offending men. The law cuts both ways. Feel free to tell a woman that she is sexually harassing you, and expect her to quit just as you would expect a man to.

The following specific definitions of harassment addressed by the US Air Force might help you to identify and clarify your understanding:

Physical Contact: *Squeezing a worker's shoulder or putting a hand around his or her waist.*

Gestures: *Puckering one's lips suggestively or making obscene signs with one's fingers or hands.*

[2]"Facts About Sexual Harassment," EEOC on line, last modified January, 1997.

Jokes: *Telling off-color, ethnic or racial jokes.*

Pictures: *Pin-ups, particularly those of scantily-clad individuals.*

Comments:*Generalities that lump one group together and denigrate them.*

Terms of Endearment: *Calling a coworker "Honey," "Dear," "Sweetheart," or some similar expression. The effect is the primary issue rather than intent. Even if the person "means nothing to you" or you have "used the term for years," you should be aware that these expressions are inappropriate.*

Questionable Compliments: *"Nice legs!" "You look hot in that outfit!" Compliments like these can make individuals feel uncomfortable or worse. Even if the person who received the "compliment" is not disturbed by it, others may be.[3]*

No matter what does or doesn't happen at work, remember that our goal as disciples, male or female, is not to humiliate, to ignore or to distrust other people, male or female. Our goal is not even to make sure we are treated well. Our goals are (1) for people "to be saved and to come to a knowledge of the truth" and (2) to live in a way that "will make the teaching about God our Savior attractive" to them.[4]

∽

Certainly, maintaining purity is not the only goal in our relationships with men at work. Together we do have jobs to accomplish:

---

[3] "Discrimination and Sexual Harassment," US Air Force on line, October 1995.
[4] 1 Timothy 2: 4; Titus 2:10

concepts to develop, patients to heal, scripts to learn, students to teach, machines to fix, products to sell and clients to serve. We can be friends with the men at work as long as we are wise. If you remember, many of the examples of evangelistic "success stories" in Chapter 5 were men who became Christians because women shared with them. Additionally, some of the communication and team-playing aspects of male/female relationships at work are covered in Chapter 7. But, I did devote this whole chapter to the subject of purity for obvious reasons: The difference between the sexes introduces inherent power and possible problems in any societal arena—especially the workplace.

In relationships with men:

Warm but wise.

Bold but gentle.

Discerning but trusting.

Humble but confident.

Helpful but careful.

Is it any wonder we need the power of the Holy Spirit

every day?

A Fresh Cup of Life

Those of you who started working before more stringent laws had been passed about sexual harassment, think back through your work-life. Do you remember experiences of harassment that were never dealt with? Do you carry any hurt or resentment because of these? If so, talk with someone and get everything cleared out. Forgive and move on.

Is anyone at work currently acting inappropriately toward you in any way? If yes, how will you deal with it?

What are your personal convictions about keeping your work relationships with men totally pure?

What temptations have you encountered at work? Have you been open about them with another Christian woman?

What is the best way that you can reach out to share your faith with the men at your workplace?

We want to live a life that
produces an abundant crop of the fresh
fruit of the Spirit—bushel baskets
and truckloads.

CHAPTER 7

Together

Being a Team Player

"Set it up next time!" yelled a red-faced guy in the front row as the volleyball sailed six feet beyond the back line. He was addressing a girl directly behind him—the one with the bandanna and sheepish look. He had been eagerly awaiting a spike opportunity when she one-armed the ball into orbit. She silently prayed that the ball would not come to her again because she had no clue how to "set it up." Since she did not know how to work with the team, she had several options: keep on doing her own thing and get yelled at, quit the team or learn the skills needed to be a team player.

But what about the "spiker" in the first row? He was the traveling sort. You know, the type who knocks you over screaming, "Mine!!" In fact, if he had his way, every ball would be his. He saw himself as the savior of the team, a one-man volleyball machine. If the team lost, it was bandanna-girl's fault. If the team won, he did it single-handedly.

Teamwork wins volleyball games, or at least brings the group closer to winning them. Harmony of purpose and focus propels a team forward. If any member lacks the needed skills, the team suffers. If any member is out for his or her own glory, the team suffers. If any member doesn't really care whether they win or lose, the team also suffers.

As women, we need to learn a lot about teamwork. Some of us have played team sports through the years, but not the majority of us. For the most part, men understand more about teamwork and the camaraderie of group activities. Women understand more about relationships and getting into the hearts and lives of individuals. Certainly both skills are needed on the job and in life in general. In this particular chapter we will focus on the skill of being a team player.

Which fruit of the spirit must we develop in order to be a valuable player on the company team? What can we learn about communicating as a member of the team?

Fruit of the Spirit

But the fruit of the Spirit is love, joy, peace, patience, kindness, goodness, faithfulness, gentleness and self-control. Against such things there is no law. Those who belong to Christ Jesus have crucified the sinful nature with its passions and desires. Since we live by the Spirit, let us keep in step with the Spirit. Let us not become conceited, provoking and envying each other (Galatians 5:22-26).

As we throng into work every day, we are to be a surrendered lot—women who have made the decision to belong to Christ Jesus.

Women who have crucified the sinful nature. Women whose passions and desires reflect those of the one we follow. We set our course every morning to speak how Jesus would speak, to feel hurts he would feel, to be bold when he would be bold, to be silent when he would be silent. We set our gait to walk in step with the Spirit. We are determined not to be conceited and focused on ourselves, not to provoke others to sin because of our lack of love, and not to envy others if they have or do what we want to have or do. In short, we want to live a life that produces an abundant crop of the fresh fruit of the Spirit—bushel baskets and truckloads.

Pick a fruit, any fruit. We need them all to live as Jesus would. But, for our purposes, we will choose three qualities that will particularly produce a spirit of teamwork on the job: patience, faithfulness and self-control.

Patience

Just to say the word "patience" is to feel *comforted* and *challenged* at the same time. We love to experience it, but we chafe at practicing it. Let's just be totally up-front: People sometimes drive us crazy, don't they? The man who clips his nails during the sales meeting. The woman who wears the jangling jewelry that jangles your nerves. The person in the next cubicle who listens to country music when your "sensitive" ears long for classical. The supervisor who taps his foot and makes a clucking noise every time he is called upon to make a decision. Need I go on? The guy with the purple hair. The girl with the shrill laugh. The balding accountant who smells of mildew, mothballs and tobacco. The person who spits in your eye while talking to you. The woman who eats her Buffalo wings to the bone and lines them up beside her plate on the table.

Have you ever stopped to think about why people get on our nerves? Are they really doing anything so terrible?

Could the reason be

that he or she

simply

is not

me?

We tolerate our own habits quite well, don't we? They don't bother us at all: Leave the top off the toothpaste? *No problem; I was in a hurry.* Pick at food in my teeth? *Of course, it was annoying me. My tongue was driving me crazy going over and over it.* How about forgetting to do an assignment at work? *It happens to everybody. I was really busy.* Someone is annoyed by any of these things? *What's her problem?*

Patience is a virtue designed for grandmothers and purple dinosaurs, we think. Think again. Patience is a fruit of the Spirit that we must be humble enough to go after. The opposite of being patient is being easily irritated. The more we are focused on ourselves, the more easily irritated we are by others. And the more we are easily irritated by others, the less we are able to love them.

The next time someone annoys you with a habit or a charac-
teristic or a mistake, remember your own humanity. And smile.
Just smile. Put yourself back into perspective as a part of the universe, not the center of it. Then allow the Spirit within to help you
overlook what you find so annoying. If you then need to bring
correction or to speak the truth in love, you will do it with a spirit
of patience. You will be like Jesus—the one who became flesh and
lived among the annoyances of those who were also flesh.

Faithfulness

Another word for "faithfulness," especially on the job, is "loyalty." Our first loyalty is to God; all other types of loyalty grow
from this primary taproot in our hearts. At work we are loyal to
our coworkers, to our companies and to our supervisors, as our
loyalty to God directs and dictates. We do not simply "clock in,"
do our thing and then get back to our "real life." Wherever we are
is our real life. If we are not faithful and loyal with what God gives
us to do and to be at work, how will we be faithful and loyal with
anything else he gives us? Jesus spoke about this in Matthew 25:21:

> "His master replied, 'Well done, good and faithful servant! You
> have been faithful with a few things; I will put you in charge of
> many things. Come and share your master's happiness!'"

Consider a first-century household servant who might have
reasoned, "I will do what my master says to a point, but obeying
exactly what he says is not that crucial. After all, my spiritual life is
my real life. Obeying God, praying and loving others is really what's

important. Sharing my faith and getting people to church is what it's all about. I mean, who cares whether the wash is done today or tomorrow? Life is not clothes; it is doing the will of God."

To him Paul said,

Slaves, obey your earthly masters in everything; and do it, not only when their eye is on you and to win their favor, but with sincerity of heart and reverence for the Lord. Whatever you do, work at it with all your heart, as working for the Lord, not for men, since you know that you will receive an inheritance from the Lord as a reward. It is the Lord Christ you are serving (Colossians 3:22-24).

What is Paul saying to us?

Obey and show respect and loyalty to your employer, not just to get a raise or a promotion. But do it out of a sincere heart that simply wants to please God. Whatever you do at work, no matter how seemingly unimportant in the overall scheme of life, do it with all your heart; do it excellently. Do it as if you were reporting to Jesus himself...because you are. And, trust me, the incentive award God has prepared for you is to die for!

In reference specifically to loyalty to your boss, consider the following suggestions:

• Part of your job is to set him/her up for success. Don't worry about whether you are getting the credit or not. When you signed on the dotted line, there was no clause guaranteeing your being given credit for every mistake of his/hers that you catch or for every idea of yours that he/she uses.

- Make every effort to accomplish what you are assigned. Say no only when it involves an issue of integrity or when it is an impossibility. (See Chapters 3 and 4.)

- Learn his/her communication and organizational style. Accept them and work with them.

- Do not try to change him/her unless he/she asks for your help. (If he/she is married, his/her spouse is doing enough of that!)

- Be careful in what you say to others regarding him/her. Just as a husband's heart should safely trust in his wife, a boss' heart should be able to safely trust in his/her employee.

- Give respect even when it seems undeserved.[1]

- Realize that there can be challenges in working for either a man or a woman. Several women have told me that they would rather work for men because they are less emotional and not as easily threatened. But, on the other hand, a male boss could tend toward being demeaning, chauvinistic or patronizing. The point is, no matter who your boss is or what his/her weaknesses are, be faithful and loyal as long as you have the job. Remember, Jesus is really your boss.

Self-Control

Bite the tongue, not the brownie. That is, be disciplined not only in what you say, but in what you eat. Watch your life, your doctrine, your words and your diet closely. Discipline in all areas

[1] 1 Peter 2:18-25

affects your spirituality and your witness. A lack of self-control hurts the team because it emphasizes the desires of the individual.

> I want to say this, so I say it.
> I want to do this, so I do it.
> I want to eat this, so I eat it.

When we are selfish in our approach, the basic "check" is "Do I want to?" not "Is it best for the team?" If we are not self-controlled in one area, it spills over generously into other areas. A lack of self-control takes away our focus and our discipline to accomplish a goal.

In order to work together we need to focus on what is best for the group. Recently, we were called to repentance in a staff meeting. (We are all disciples so we can do that!) We had begun to slip and slide in our discipline: getting to work late, not following up quickly and excellently on assignments, being vague as to why we had not followed through on projects, etc. What a joy it was simply to repent. How much better we felt about the jobs we had committed ourselves to. How much closer and more responsible we felt to each other as coworkers. Granted, most of us cannot experience wholesale repentance in our staff meetings at work, but we can experience it in our staff meetings with God, Jesus and the Holy Spirit every morning before work. We can also share our repentance with other Christians who are in the same "boat" in other "lakes."

Many of us naturally tend to think, *It's okay for me to be late. I have good reasons.* We should think, *I am no special case. I am part of the team. We all need to be here on time.* Have you ever noticed how many people are three to five minutes late and are clutching a Dunkin' Donuts or Starbucks coffee cup? *I want it, so I will get it. It won't make me that late.* Are we thinking self or team? Do we ever even consider denying ourselves something because getting it will make us late to work?

In most situations, we tend to want to be in control. We want to sit in the catbird seat. We want to call the shots. To use a sports analogy, we want to be the quarterback, the pass receiver, the coach and the commentator. *Then there would be little chance for failure,* or so we think. Part of self-control is giving over the need to control. It is playing the role we are called to play and letting others play their roles. It has to do with submission and trust and surrender.

In Jesus' "meeting" with God in Gethsemane, Jesus had an idea: Maybe there was another way to accomplish the goal without his having to die and be separated from God. He brought up his idea with passion and confidence. But the executive decision was, "I appreciate your input, but we will go with the plan as previously decided." His response was not to quit, not to emotionally pull away from working with God to accomplish the goal. He submitted to God and gave his total support to carrying out the plan— even to death on a cross.[2] And as we submit to the authorities in our lives, we are submitting to God with that same spirit. Paul puts it this way:

> Everyone must submit himself to the governing authorities, for there is no authority except that which God has established. The

[2] Philippians 2:8

authorities that exist have been established by God. Consequently, he who rebels against the authority is rebelling against what God has instituted, and those who do so will bring judgment on themselves (Romans 13:1-2).

Communication

Communication is a tricky thing. Did you say what you meant? Did he hear what you said? And what did he mean when he said what you thought he said? Words come from our mouths and build either bridges or roadblocks to understanding.

At some point, most firms and school faculties have communication specialists come in and do a seminar helping people to identify their communication styles. In the school where I worked, a diagram was displayed prominently in the teachers' lounge. It was divided into four sections, each representing a different communication style. Each teacher had written his or her name in the section that most closely fits his or her style. The purpose was to help them communicate in a way that they would most easily be understood.

Mr. "Smith" liked very direct communication. Don't beat around the bush. Don't buffer what you say. Just get down to it quickly. Bottom line, that's what he wanted.

But, Mrs. "White" needed more explanation and more warning when something difficult was to be said. She needed plenty of affirmation. Bottom line, yes. But not too quickly.

This type of exercise is helpful if people are indeed interested in being sensitive to each other's needs. As Christians we certainly should be trying to communicate in the best possible way with our coworkers. The better we get to know them, the better we can communicate with them—male or female, manager or managee.

Harmful Communication

Communication is an ongoing challenge in any group. To know that communication between the two sexes is an added challenge, all you have to do is see some of the best sellers over the past few years like *Men Are from Mars, Women Are from Venus.*[3] In fact, all you really have to do as a woman is to communicate with a man for any period of time. The communication gap will be obvious.

As women we have good tendencies and bad tendencies in our communication. Let's look first at three of the bad ones we need to avoid, especially when communicating with men: being hesitant, harsh and hysterical. (Please excuse me in this chapter if I seem to stereotype women; although I am one, you know! I am dealing with general tendencies, not absolutes.)

Hesitant

Mary had a great idea about raising productivity in a certain area of the business. She thought about it. She rethought about it. She considered it from all angles. When a kink showed up, she untied it and adjusted her conclusions.

When the day of the staff meeting arrived, so did Mary, along

[3] John Gray, *Men Are from Mars, Women Are from Venus* (New York: HarperCollins, 1992).

with five others who also had great plans to raise productivity. When it was her turn to give her suggestion, she said, "This might not work, or you might have thought of this already. It might take some tweaking to implement...."

It was an excellent plan, but the others in the group never even heard it. They had already stopped listening after her second qualifier. They completely dismissed her input.

Some women want to be taken seriously in their work situations, but their desire to please others and to protect themselves makes them tentative, apologetic and hesitant in their input. They fail to realize that they are valuable assets to the team, and by right of being on the team, they do have a say in the decision process. Their perspective and insight are needed as part of the synergy of the group.

Sometimes in our fear of sounding haughty, we revert to sounding hesitant. Through the Spirit within, we can be confident and secure rather than haughty or hesitant. God is in control. If our ideas are shot down, it does not mean that *we* are being shot down. We should not take interactions so personally. We must invest in our ideas, but not find our identity or worth in them. A valuable employee is one who thinks critically, but is a team player. He or she can both give and take strong, thoughtful input.

Paul tells us that because of our faith in Jesus "we may approach God with freedom and confidence" (Ephesians 3:12). If we can confidently approach the God who is the Creator, Sustainer and Culminater of the universe, surely we can approach people at work with just a little more certainty.

Harsh

Many of us find dealing with conflict difficult. We put it off. We ignore it. We try to act *sweet* on the outside, but on the inside our stomachs churn around deeply embedded pits. So we summon up our courage, take a deep breath and spit it out. *There! I've done it,* we think. Yet, the *way* we did it was not encouraging or gentle. It was really more like throwing up verbally. It was harsh and grating. Maybe even shrill because of the tremendous emotion embodied in our words.

It does take a lot of "umph" to get over the hump of fear when conflict is possible and/or probable. We need to pray for God's strength to say what we need to say and to say it in a godly way.

Men hate to be scolded by women. It makes them feel how they felt when Mom or Aunt Susan fussed at them for getting their new pants dirty. Women have the natural "ability" to be abrasive, biting and critical—thus, Shakespeare's play *The Taming of the Shrew*. Proverbs reminds us that "a gentle answer turns away wrath, but a harsh word stirs up anger" (Proverbs 15:1). And Peter reminds us to have "the unfading beauty of a gentle and quiet spirit, which is of great worth in God's sight" (1 Peter 3:4). Let's speak the truth and be faithful, but let's do it in a way that helps the other person hear clearly what we are saying.

If I am upset with someone at work, it helps me to run it by someone else. To "run it by" protects me from "running over" the person I'm upset with. If I talk out some of the emotion before actually confronting the person, I can more evenly and gently express my concerns.

We have all seen and known (and probably been) women who appear cold and unfeeling. They have blocked and denied their emotions, and the result is hardness and harshness. As women, God gives us the capacity to be soft and to be nurturing. Let's not give away such a gift for any reason.

Hysterical

Emotions are powerful. They move deeply within us and motivate us for good or for evil. God gave us emotions so that we could experience his nature. They are a gift, a blessing. But sometimes we think of them as a curse—especially when we are having great difficulty controlling them. We think, *I would rather not have emotions. All they do is get me into trouble.* But, the truth is, if we did not have them, we would not be able to appreciate the beauty of a sunset. We would not be free to experience love for our families. We would not be equipped to shed tears of sorrow or joy. We would not really want to be without emotions; they are essential to experiencing life to the full.

So, we've got them and unless we medicate ourselves to get rid of them, we will continue to have them. The trick is to control them…or to let God control them.

In my own personal experience I have found that men listen more carefully and take more seriously what I am saying if I am not overly emotional (and certainly if I am not hysterical). If we have problems in work situations, we need to take the time to think them through logically and pray about them before we start shooting off our mouths. Don't complain or whine. Figure out why the situations are not best for the team or why they hamper your productivity. These kinds of bottom lines communicate to management and coworkers. They also validate your concerns and indicate that you are looking for solutions to actual problems and not just complaining. Remember Paul's injunction to the Philippian disciples:

> Do everything without complaining or arguing, so that you may become blameless and pure, children of God without fault in a crooked and depraved generation, in which you shine like stars in the universe as you hold out the word of life...(Philippians 2:14-16).

Helpful Communication

Jesus reminded us that when bad is swept out, good must re-place it.[4] As we sweep out hesitant, harsh and hysterical communication, we must usher in honest, humble and harmonious communication.

Honest

> An honest answer
> is like a kiss on the lips (Proverbs 24:26).

In Chapter 3 we dealt with honesty at length. I mention it here simply because it starts with an "h." No, really, I just want to emphasize that out of the fear of being harsh or hysterical, we might pull away from being honest. But as the previous proverb indicates, it is through being honest that we truly show love and affection to

---

[4] Matthew 12:43-45

our coworkers. When I have on my "writer" hat, I appreciate the other editors here at DPI for giving me honest input. For instance, they might tell me that I should remove the second sentence in this paragraph. I enjoyed writing it, but I need their input as to whether to leave it in or not. (Yea! I got to keep it.) Honesty is important in order to do any job well. As an employee, we owe honesty to our employers; as a worker, we owe honesty to our coworkers.

Humble

Humble is not Milquetoast. It is not weak, frail, impotent or spineless. Humble is strong, controlled, healthy, teachable and secure. Humble communication first and foremost desires

- to know what is right, not just to *be* right;
- to affirm and build others up, not to cause them to look or feel less;
- to understand first, not to be understood;
- to cause others to feel competent, appreciated and needed, not to exaggerate one's own importance.

Paul sums up the spirit of humility:

Do nothing out of selfish ambition or vain conceit, but in humility consider others better than yourselves (Philippians 2:3).

Miriam was a woman who forgot the power of a humble heart and of humble communication. (Do remember that the heart is a prerequisite to the communication.) Her brother Moses was referred to by God as the most humble man on the face of the earth.

Even while being led by such a man, she became full of her own importance and exaggerated the extent of her role: "Has the Lord spoken only through Moses?" she and her brother Aaron asked, "Hasn't he also spoken through us?" Since Miriam was the one God inflicted with leprosy, it is my guess that she was the ringleader of the two. (Read their story in Numbers 12.)

Whoever we work for or with, it is safe to say that he or she is not the most humble person on the face of the earth. We will certainly be at least as tempted as Miriam was to communicate in a prideful way. Let's learn from our sister: God is not pleased with prideful hearts and prideful communication, and neither builds "team."

Paul's words to Titus could serve as our hallmark in the workplace. We are "to be obedient, to be ready to do whatever is good, to slander no one, to be peaceable and considerate, and to show true humility toward all men" (Titus 3:1b-2).

Harmonious

Have you ever sat next to a person who sings off-key? If you know anything about music, then you know about chords. Certain notes harmonize to form those chords. Any two or more of those notes played together will produce harmony. But if a wrong note is played, disharmony or dissonance results.

When I study Galatians 5:19-21 with someone to help her become convicted about her sin, I always give the following definition for "discord": Discord is when you know which note is the right one, but you purposely play the wrong one. It's when you know what you could say that would encourage the person or resolve the situation, and you purposely do not say it. Pride. Stubbornness. Rebellion. They're all in there. And they all destroy unity and team.

Whether at home or at work, harmonious communication is wholesome communication that "is helpful for building others up according to their needs, that it may benefit those who listen" (Ephesians 4:29).

❧

Jesus is certainly an expert in training and producing team players. The church for whom he died is his "team." We personally are all players on his team. Our daily ministry involves teamwork with other disciples. As Paul put it:

> I planted the seed, Apollos watered it, but God made it grow. So neither he who plants nor he who waters is anything, but only God, who makes things grow. The man who plants and the man who waters have one purpose, and each will be rewarded according to his own labor. For we are God's fellow workers; you are God's field, God's building (1 Corinthians 3:5-9).

The better we understand our roles as fellow workers on God's team, the better we will understand our roles on our teams at work—and the more we will be like Jesus at work.

A Fresh Cup of Life

Would the people at work say you are a team player?

Would your ministry leader say you are a team player? To make sure your view is accurate, ask him or her.

In what ways do you need to grow in order to be a better team player?

Of the three types of Spirit-fruit mentioned, in which are you strongest and in which are you weakest? (patience, faithfulness and self-control)

Do you tend to be hesitant, harsh or hysterical in your communication at work? Think through your harmful communication tendencies and how you can change them.

Do you tend to be honest, humble and harmonious in your communication at work? Think through your helpful communication tendencies and how you can improve them.

The heart of the commute is determined
by the heart of the commuter.

Chapter 8

ℰ

On the Road Again

An Encouraging Commute

Rush-hour traffic. Every woman for herself. Every man for himself. Speed up. Slow down. Blow the horn. Bite the tongue. Avoid the eyes. The asphalt jungle teems with beasts today.

Regina readied herself for the battle, picking up her sword and shield. The jungle awaited her entry. Wild animals circled the rotary and hunkered at intersections—ready to pounce, ready to badger, ready to torment.

The guy in the little blue Camaro thinks he owns the road; I'll show him. I won't let him in....I can't believe it! The nerve of that guy! He came in anyway!! Yeah, he tips his hand to say thanks. Thanks for what? I didn't let you in; you barged in.

What does that woman think she is doing? Get off my tail, lady! Where's the fire?

Whoa! Wait a minute! she says to herself. *Where is that gentle and quiet spirit you read about and prayed for today? Where are those clothes of "compassion, kindness, humility, gentleness and patience" that you* put on this morning?[1] *Have they so quickly come off? Are you driving to work dressed in "anger, rage and malice"? Girl, you better make a quick change; you've got the wrong clothes on!*

⁓

With a little imagination consider the prophet Nahum's description of rush-hour traffic:

> An attacker advances against you, Nineveh [your name].
> > Guard the fortress,
> > watch the road,
> > brace yourselves,
> > marshal all your strength! (Nahum 2:1).

Isn't this how you feel some mornings? You see the other drivers, especially the aggressive ones, as attackers advancing against you.

We know well the "way of the jungle." But do we know well the way of Jesus in the jungle? John tells us that Jesus himself is the "road" to God (*odos* in John 14:6). He who is the road will teach us the way of the road. Jesus came not to be served, but to serve. Do you think of yourself as a servant to other drivers? Paul said that we have a "continuing debt to love one another" (Romans 13:8). That means we owe it to other drivers to love them.

This is not an insignificant issue. How much good does it do to have a great quiet time followed by a sinful commute to the office? What kind of shape will you be in when you arrive? How

[1] Colossians 3:12

well are you handling the "test of the road"? Are you handling it as Jesus would? Ask yourself the following questions to evaluate your "road spirituality":

- When someone is having a rough time entering the flow of traffic, do you let him in? Or do you speed up and avoid eye contact, acting as though you didn't realize he wanted in?

- Do you talk at or yell at other drivers who are rude and inconsiderate, either out loud or in your mind? Or do you say, "Father, forgive them. They do not know what they are doing"?

- Are you at peace when traffic jams are making you late? Do you say to yourself, "God is in control. Ranting, venting and fuming will not change a thing"? "Peace! Be still!" is still said to us by Jesus, and he is not talking about the weather—he is talking about our hearts.

- Do you ever think about what is happening in the lives of the other drivers? *Maybe the reason he is so rude is that no one has ever really been kind to him. Maybe her husband hit her before she left the house today. Maybe his mother is dying of cancer.* Surely Jesus looks at those in traffic jams and has compassion on them, because they are "harassed and helpless, like sheep without a shepherd" (Matthew 9:36).

Christlike attitudes see us through challenging commutes with stop-and-go traffic. They allow us to arrive at work without feeling the need to strangle the first unwitting persons we see. They erase the glazed look from our eyes. They help us to "bear with" and to "forgive" others, even on the way to work (Colossians 3:13).

A writer who has been an inspiration to me through the years is Amy Carmichael, a missionary to India in the early 1900s. The following is a sample of her pithy and insightful comments:

A cup brimful of sweet water cannot spill even one drop of bitter water however suddenly jolted.[2]

So, fill it to the brim, with God and his Word every day. Pull out onto the highway with confidence and a gentle and quiet spirit. And when you are jolted, spill out only sweet water.

Foundational Attitudes

Hear, O Israel: The Lord our God, the Lord is one. Love the Lord your God with all your heart and with all your soul and with all your strength. These commandments that I give you today are to be upon your hearts. Impress them on your children. *Talk about them when you sit at home and when you walk along the road*, when you lie down and when you get up. Tie them as symbols on your hands and bind them on your foreheads. Write them on the door-frames of your houses and on your gates (Deuteronomy 6: 4-9, emphasis added).

God understands that we live in a day-to-day world. He understood that the Israelites did also. He gave practical instructions to help them to see how following his Word fit into their everyday lives. In the above passage he tells parents to take advantage of the time with their children "on the road." They were told to first put on their hearts the commandments of God and then to "impress

---

[2] Amy Carmichael, *If* (Christian Literature Crusade: Fort Washington, Pennsylvania, 1938), 46.

these commandments" upon their children. If you do have your children with you on the way to work, take advantage of the time to sing spiritual songs and to talk to them about what is facing them that day. Help them to see how God fits into their day.

Marcie, a single mom who is an executive secretary, shared how she uses her time with her two daughters on the way to work:

> My daughters and I sing and pray on our commute in. On our commute home, we talk about "the three best things that God allowed to happen today and how they made me feel."

For the rest of us who do not have children with us when we drive to work: Get the message of this passage. It is not only instructional for parents with children. It tells us that our hearts must be fully and firstly and fiercely devoted to God. The end. Bottom line. We must have this foundation in our lives before we do anything else—even before we start our commutes. (Remember Chapter 1 about our daily walk with God.) We are to be spiritually minded whether we have children with us or not. If we don't start off with desiring to please God and with asking for his help in doing so, we will not make it very far into our days without blowing it.

No Self-Centered Thinking

"An idle mind is the devil's workshop." If you drive by yourself to work, do you allow your mind to idle along with your car? I find it very easy to waste the thirty to forty-five minutes when I commute by myself. My thinking can wander, and if I am not careful, it can become self-focused.

Would you believe that Jesus had to rebuke his disciples for their self-centered thinking during their "commute" together to Capernaum?

> ...he asked them, "What were you arguing about on the road?" But they kept quiet because on the way they had argued about who was the greatest (Mark 9:33-34).

Human nature is human nature, whether walking dusty roads in sandaled feet or driving sixty-five miles per hour on the interstate.

If we find our minds in neutral, we have to decide to put them into drive (or first gear for those with "standard-shift" brains). Do you ride the train or the subway and let your mind drift into self-centered thinking: ways people at work have hurt you, a cute come-back you could have used earlier, the annoying habits of a workmate, the fact that no one understands how much you have to do or how unfair your company policies are?

Paul admonished the Philippians to "do everything without arguing and complaining." Like the disciples on the road, when we are self-centered, we begin to argue and complain, (even if it is inside our heads). We bemoan the problems instead of looking for solutions. We focus on the negatives to the eclipse of the positives. This is not a mind-set out of which grows hope, love and the desire to make a difference in the lives of others at work. The heart of the commute is determined by the heart of the commuter.

Several women shared their others-focused approach to driving to and from work:

It's a great quiet time. I usually spend it thinking about what I'm going to do with my family and church, and I pray.

-Charlotte

I try to ride with other disciples who work with me or near me. This is great because we can encourage each other before work.

-Mindy

...listening to tapes, making a grateful list on the way to work, allowing myself six or seven [calls] on the cellular on the way home!

-Charlene

My husband and I are committed to commuting once a week and try for twice a week together. This has been the highlight of the week because I get the extra twenty minutes in the morning with him. The travel time is often our best time to plan the week and discuss the needs to address.

-Elaine

Those who ride the train or the subway must also discover ways to be others-focused:

I try to talk to people as I travel on the T [subway train]. I love to hear about people's lives. One thing I've been trying to do is not to worry right away about how to share with the person, but to just talk and let God direct the conversation.

-Gwendellyn

I try to share with someone at least on every subway I ride. I strike up a conversation with whoever sits beside me and invite them to church or to study. I have made many friends and met souls later saved this way! It also gets me outward focused for the day ahead.

-Julie

Two commuting temptations are reading and listening to a walkman. At one point I was reading one-plus books a week on the subway. I did not even *see* who sat beside me! (Seventy-five percent of those on the bus or train are reading or have earplugs in their ears. Self-focus entirely.) Now, I take my Bible, which starts conversations.

-Mary Ann

I appreciate these women and so many just like them who are willing to overcome their selfish, self-focused desires and give to others, whether they are actually with people or by themselves.

Give Thought to Our Ways

Although we must not be self-centered in our thinking, we do need to be reflective and evaluative. The commute is a good time to take stock. On the way to work ask yourself specific questions: How determined am I to rely on God today? What will I face that I will particularly need God's help with? What is my focus-thought for the day? And then on the way home: What was the challenge that was the most difficult for me today? How well did I handle it? What will be the needs of my family when I get home? How can I prepare myself to give to my family or roommates even though I am tired?

A wicked man puts up a bold front,
  but an upright man gives thought to his ways
    (Proverbs 21:29).

The wisdom of the prudent is to give thought to their ways,
  but the folly of fools is deception (Proverbs 14:8).

So, if we are upright ("marked by strong moral rectitude") and prudent ("marked by wisdom"), we will give thought to our ways. We will not just assume that we are doing great. How easy it is to get into a rut of superficiality as we drive to and from work day after day. How much more exciting to go after more adventure in our relationship with God, to give thought to our ways and to pray that God will help us to grow and change.

Spiritually Focused

What are some ways to help ourselves stay spiritually focused while driving to and from work?

- **Prayer**—At the very top of this list must be prayer. Talking to God. Sharing your thoughts, fears, feelings, joys and convictions. He loves to hear from us, and we need to talk to him. I might add, though, that we should not rely solely on "drive-by" prayers. We also need time to enter our "closets" or to be out in nature and not have to be watching the road.

- **The Bible on tape**—Remember when the two disciples were walking and talking with Jesus on the road to Emmaus? After he left them, they said to each other, "Were not our hearts burning within us while he talked with us on the road and opened the Scriptures to us?" (Luke 24:32). Did you get that? He talked to them on the road. No matter how many times you have read certain books of the Bible, when you hear them read on tape, you will hear something new. Jesus once again talks to his disciples on the road, and his words continue to cause our hearts to burn within us nearly two centuries later.

- **Sermon and class tapes**—We, like the Ethiopian, can ponder God's word while riding in our "chariots." Philip came along to help him understand God's word.[3] I don't advise that we pick up hitchhikers to help us understand the Bible, but tapes by others can help us in the same way. Many tape sets are available on a variety of subjects from the study of books of the Bible to overcoming difficult situations in our lives. Several people could buy different tape sets and share them with each other.

- **Singing spiritual songs**—Don't be concerned about looking stupid to others; at least they cannot *hear* you! You see people all the time rocking out to songs on the radio. Why shouldn't you rock out too? Rejoice with the psalmist: "I will sing to the Lord all my life; I will sing praise to my God as long as I live" (Psalm 104:33).

- **Listening to spiritual music**—Whether spiritual "oldie-goldies" or current Christian music, music regenerates the soul. That's why Saul had David play the harp for him when he was down and depressed. Music can wake us up and get us going. It can also put us in a contemplative mood and draw us nearer to the heart of God. Through others we can hear God singing to us.[4]

- **Friends on tape**—When we discussed this topic of having an encouraging commute in our 9-to-5 group, we decided to make a cassette tape for each other. Each person took a few minutes to share a scripture and comment on tape to encourage her sisters. Then I made copies for everyone. As I played my tape, I felt as though all those women were riding to work with me. It was unifying and bonding! (As I write about it, I realize that we should do it again.)

[3] Acts 8:24-40
[4] Zephaniah 3:17

- **You on tape**—My husband has Multiple Sclerosis and suffers extreme fatigue, especially during the late afternoon. As he would drive home from work, he found himself having many negative thoughts about himself and his ability to do all that needed to be done. When he would drive to work in the morning, his mind was fresher and his thoughts more focused. So for several weeks, he recorded his morning thoughts and prayers and played them back to himself during the afternoon ride. It helped him to keep a positive perspective and to keep his thoughts focused on God's power during his personal times of weakness.

(If you ride a train or subway, many of these suggestions are also helpful. Just remember to take your headphones off long enough to meet someone!)

Make a Decision

Apart from using it sinfully, there is no right or wrong way to use your commute time. However you use it, though, let it be because you made a decision. You may decide that you simply need some quiet time with your mind at rest. Amen! But guard against being lazy-minded and not giving any real thought about how you want to spend the time.

Some disciples listen to the news or talk radio. They want to get the pulse of the times. Christians sometimes live in a religious bubble and don't know what's going on in the world around them. One brother who listens to talk radio said that he became convicted that he should know more about current events because Jesus did. He referenced Jesus in Luke 13:1-4:

Now there were some present at that time who told Jesus about the Galileans whose blood Pilate had mixed with their sacrifices. Jesus answered, "Do you think that these Galileans were worse sinners than all the other Galileans because they suffered this way? I tell you, no! But unless you repent, you too will all perish. Or those eighteen who died when the tower in Siloam fell on them—do you think they were more guilty than all the others living in Jerusalem?"

Jesus knew what was happening around him, and he used those current events to make a spiritual point with people.

Between her commute and working with the teen ministry in her area, one of our editorial assistants spends as much as three or four hours a day in her car. Although she prays often, she still has a great deal of time available and was searching for other constructive pursuits. She has decided to buy or rent or borrow books on tape, which will help her stay abreast of current books and sharpen her editing skills. She also listens to current music so she will know more about what the teens are hearing.

One more decision that will set you up for a more encouraging commute is to *leave on time*. Figure out the optimum time at which you need to walk out of your house in order to be at work five minutes early. It is amazing how much better my time on the road is if I feel relaxed. If I leave late, the commute is consumed with my saying to myself, *Why didn't I leave sooner? I've got to hurry! I can shave a few minutes off by turning here. Everybody's in my way.* I find it very hard to focus on anything meaningful when I'm running behind. Also if I leave in time and I am truly delayed by a traffic jam or construction, I don't feel guilty because I am giving my best and being responsible.

Hopefully from this chapter you have been given encouragement and direction and possibilities that will cause you to evaluate how you are spending your time and to make the best use of it. Some of the suggestions take planning ahead, and some are more spontaneous. But however you choose to spend the time, don't see your commute as an enemy; see it as a friend. No matter how long or how far you commute, be sure to always stay on the narrow road, the highway of holiness:

> And a highway will be there;
>   it will be called the Way of Holiness.
> The unclean will not journey on it;
>   it will be for those who walk in that Way;
> wicked fools will not go about on it (Isaiah 35:8).

After all, we are all commuting to heaven—our real home!

A Fresh Cup of Life

What are your greatest joys, frustrations and temptations during your commute?

How has reading this chapter helped you have a more godly view of your commute?

How full of "sweet water" is your cup on the way to or from work? How can you sweeten the water?

What one new approach to commuting do you want to try this week?

Only from the vantage point of the altar
can God's will be clearly seen.

CHAPTER 9

_ᐛ_

To Change
or Not to Change

What If I Do Not Like My Job?

Francie glanced at the gas gauge. *Almost on empty. Why didn't I fill up last night when there was no traffic?* she thought as she pulled into the gas station.

Someone had left an Oldsmobile with the motor running, blocking both pumps. Finally an older lady walked slowly around the car, got in and parked beside the restroom. Francie got a quick five dollars' worth of gas, and pulled out into the molasses-momentum traffic.

As she thought about the day ahead, that old familiar pit began to form in her stomach. She really hated her job. The boss was overbearing. The pressure to produce was intense. Her co-workers constantly gossiped. She felt like she was going nowhere. She had graduated from high school tenth in her class, and had gotten a degree in journalism from a well-respected university. What was she doing working in a job that used so few of her talents and so little of her training?

She reached to turn on the radio as if to drown out her thoughts. Before she could switch it from news to music, she heard something she couldn't believe. Surely her ears were lying. The newsperson was reading clearly: "There is news this morning of a merger between Mohawk and Nautical Banks. After several tries at settling upon terms, spokespersons for both banks report a satisfactory agreement. The new name has not yet been announced...."

A chill ran up her spine while anger boiled in her blood. She thought, *Surely he was wrong. This is a mistake. I've worked at Mohawk for five years. How could they do something like this without even letting us know?*

Insecurity initiated a litany of questions: *Who will stay, and who will go? Will I still have a job? Will I be demoted? Will our product be retained? Whose operating procedures will be used? What about the training class I am currently teaching? Is it all for nothing? And why do I care so much anyway since I don't really even like this job?*

Her palms were sweaty. Her head felt light and vacant. She was in a job situation in which she hated to stay but was scared to leave—a puzzling paradox to be sure.

As she pulled into the bank parking lot, she saw several co-workers getting out of their cars. *Had they just heard too? Or,* she shuddered, *did they already know? Maybe I was kept in the dark because the management plans to let me go.*

Feeling betrayed and doomed, Francie walked slowly toward the building. Lester called out, "Did you hear the news? I just heard it on the radio. What is going on?" She shrugged her shoulders, took a deep breath and walked through the doorway, bracing herself for whatever was ahead.

⁓

Have you ever thought or said, "I hate my job"? Numerous polls in the last few years have indicated that 83 to 92 percent of people in the US are not happy with their jobs. A recent survey in Japan showed roughly the same percentages.[1]

As you read the story above, did you know Francie? Are you Francie?

Downsizing, mergers, buyouts—they all cast shadows of discontent and insecurity in the job market. More and more people seem to want job security and job satisfaction even more than they want higher salaries. We have all heard of Wall Street executives who moved to Vermont to grow organic vegetables and reconnect with themselves and their families. They had decided that quality of life means more than a fat bankroll, designer suits, the latest supercharged sports car and a gigantic home in the suburbs.

But what about you, as one who has decided to follow Jesus Christ? How should you respond if you don't like your job? What kind of attitude does God want you to have? What is the difference between contentment and complacency? How is God building your

[1] Jane Boucher, *How to Love the Job You Hate* (Nashville: Thomas Nelson Publishers, 1994), 1.

character through the job? Does being underemployed bring glory to God? What about loyalty—to whom is it due? Is the grass really greener on the other side of the parking lot?

Reasons for Disliking Jobs

People give a host of reasons for not liking their jobs. Let me name a few:

- cut-throat competitiveness
- pressure to produce
- too much expected
- emphasis on bottom line
- not enough money
- inflexible and/or long hours
- worldly atmosphere
- sexual undertones
- persecution because of faith
- meaninglessness of tasks assigned
- lack of opportunity to use talent
- inept and/or uncaring management
- rude customers
- lack of cooperation
- unethical business practices

I'm sure I could go on and on...or some of you could. But take another look at the list and at any other reasons you might have added. How many of the reasons are ones that you will likely encounter in any worldly job situation? Leaving one job and going to another one will not necessarily offer a less worldly atmosphere or more competent management or less pressure to produce. On the other hand it might offer relief from rude customers, if your new job is in the archive department of the library and involves no interaction with the public. Another job situation might also offer more ethical business practices simply because the CEO has a different philosophy of operations. It is important, though, to realize which situations automatically come with the worldly work-package and to accept the challenge of that package. Then you can get on with being a shining light in a very dark world.

Discernment

How can you tell whether you simply need to be content in a difficult job situation or if you are becoming complacent and too lazy to seek a more challenging or satisfying job? Good question!

Contentment

To offer some spiritual guidance in answering this good question, let's look first at 1 Corinthians 7:17-24. (If at all possible, please stop and read the passage...even if you are settled in and your Bible is in the next room.)

Paul counsels a disciple "to remain in the situation which he was in when God called him" (7:20). Does this principle mean a disciple should never accept a promotion or apply for a higher paying job? Paul clears up any confusion about this in the next verse: "Were you a slave when you were called? Don't let it trouble you—although if you can gain your freedom, do so."

Paul is calling the Corinthian disciples to be content in their life situations, to bring glory to God in whatever path they are called to walk. They were not to envy another person's standing in the community or family fortune or freedom. As disciples came together to form the family of God, all social classes were mixed. This would have happened nowhere else in first-century society, and discontentment could have deepened as the "have-not's" became intimate friends with the "have's." The slaves and people in lower positions could have reasoned, *If we are equals and God loves us all the same, why is he blessing Rufus over there more than he is blessing me?* Discontent and envy could have disunified the church. Paul in essence says, "Be content with what you have. If you are given the chance to better your situation, take it. But if not, do not allow bitterness or resentment or envy to rob you of your faith and of a heart at peace with God. All that really matters is that you are God's servant and God's freeman."

In writing to Timothy, Paul expresses much the same thought:

> But godliness with contentment is great gain. For we brought nothing into the world, and we can take nothing out of it. But if we have food and clothing, we will be content with that. People who want to get rich fall into temptation and a trap and into many foolish and harmful desires that plunge men into ruin and destruction. For the love of money is a root of all kinds of evil. Some people, eager for money, have wandered from the faith and pierced themselves with many griefs (1 Timothy 6:6-10).

Paul is calling for a heart that is content and grateful for what God has already given. If you have a job that is less than ideal, first you must be grateful that you have a job; many do not. If you are bitter or resentful, get your heart surrendered to God before you make a job change. Otherwise, you will take your old attitude into your new job. And guess what, it won't take long in the new situation for it to pop back up again. Root out the old attitude! Then place yourself on the altar. Only from the vantage point of the altar can God's will be clearly seen.[2] You will be amazed at the ways God will bless you in your present job because of your changed mind and heart, whether he does or does not bless you in the future with a new job. One sister shared her experience with being content and with being blessed:

> I had been working in my company for twelve years when I made a job change (within the company). At the time I took the job, I was offered the opportunity to learn new skills and do interesting projects. Several months into the job, an organizational change took place within the group. The opportunities for new skills were given to others. Besides that, my coworker had a very close friendship with our boss. Other managers would cater to her opinions or concerns. I felt that my suggestions were overlooked if they were different from hers. I became very frustrated and angry. I got bad attitudes toward those managers. I was not a happy camper to say the least.
>
> My decision: I was open with my sin to others in my discipleship group. I talked to my husband about my feelings and frustrations. I began to study out scriptures like Colossians 3:23, 1 Peter 3:12-17, Genesis 4:7 and Romans 12:13. I began to pray for peace and contentment at my job.
>
> When I finally surrendered to God's will, I was able to be more objective and open-minded about my situation. With much advice and many prayers, I decided to look for another job within the company. During that time, I

[2] Romans 12:1-2

gave my heart to doing the best job I could until I found a new position. I looked for ways to use my talents with the other managers. My relationships with them improved tremendously. I began to have respect for my boss again. Also, within three months, I found another job that paid more money and offered more opportunities to learn new skills. "...in all things God works for the good of those who love him..." (Romans 8:28).

-*Earlina, 35, IM consultant*

Remember that God says to knock on the door, not to kick it down![3] Faith knocks; discontent, faithlessness and impatience work together to kick down the door. Have you ever noticed how a kicked-down door can destroy whatever good thing is on the other side? Learn with Isaiah to "wait on the Lord" and let him bless you with his answer.[4] And be content as you wait!

Complacency

Now, what about complacency? Sometimes it lurks under a cloak of contentment. How do you recognize it? You can begin to identify complacency by realizing the "company" it keeps: namely fear, laziness, negativity and a misunderstanding of putting the kingdom first. Ask yourself the following questions:

- Does my job allow me to use the talents and skills I have?
- Do I know what my talents and skills are?
- Am I willing to take on more responsibility?
- Is there anything fulfilling or satisfying about my job?
- Am I willing to take a risk in going after a new job?

[3] Matthew 7:7-8
[4] Isaiah 40:31, KJV

- Am I willing to research ways to retrain for another job?
- Am I willing to take on whatever task God calls me to do?

The more "no's" you have, the more likely it is that you are complacent rather than content. Let's look at complacency's "buddies" one at a time and blow their cover.

Fear

God gives us talents, and he expects us to discover them and to use them. Jesus' parable about the talents clearly demonstrates God's expectations in this area. (Please read Matthew 25:14-30.) God gives differing degrees of talent to people. From those to whom he gives much talent, he expects more in return. From those to whom he gives less talent, he expects a proportionate return. Notice what the one-talent servant said about his use of the talent given him by the master: "...I was afraid and went out and hid your talent in the ground. See, here is what belongs to you" (Matthew 25:25). Out of fear he buried his talent. He was unwilling to take a risk. And my guess is that he was tentative and wavering in everything else he did. He had no faith that God would bless him.

Does this ring a bell for you? Are you afraid to discover and use your talents? Are you afraid even to let yourself think about what type of job would employ your talents to a greater extent? As the saying goes, "Use them or lose them!" Taking a risk in faith, through prayer and advice, is exhilarating! It places you beyond the comfortable shoreline of complacency and into the deep waters of trust and expectation. And when you are out in those waves, Jesus comes to you and says, "Take courage! It is I. Don't be afraid" (Matthew 14:27).

Laziness

Notice that in Jesus' parable the servant identified fear in his heart, but the master nailed him on laziness, calling him a "wicked, lazy servant" (Matthew 25:26). The unwillingness to work harder and take on more responsibility is laziness, no matter why we are unwilling. A lack of faith is laziness because Jesus says that the primary work we are to do is to believe (John 6:29)!

Why should you be open to rethinking and even to retraining? Simply to use your God-given talents and to give glory to God. Your influence on non-Christians can be more far-reaching if you are joyfully using all your talents. You can give more to the church to further mission efforts if you have a better-paying job. You will have a greater sense of wholeness and confidence if you are being challenged to use your talents and skills every day. And as you develop more of your talents and skills, you will have more to offer to the ongoing functioning of the body of Christ, the church.

If laziness is indeed a buddy to complacency, it is a first cousin to apathy. And an apathetic, "I don't care" attitude leaves us dead in the water as a disciple. Don't settle for less than what God wants for you. Pray that your dreams will be a reflection of God's plans for you.

Negativity

You may realize that you should be looking for another type of job. Like Francie in the story at the beginning of the chapter, you may have training for something that is not even in the ballpark of what you are currently doing. You may be frustrated, but you may not have a clue how to go about discovering the job you should go after. Later in the chapter we will discuss some steps to help you make such a discovery. But first, test your heart. When you think about exploring other job options, do a host of negative thoughts rush to your head? Thoughts like the following: *I have no idea what type of change I need. Who would want to hire me anyway? Even if I tried, it wouldn't work out. I could never do more than I am doing. I'm not smart enough. I'm not confident enough. I'm not pretty enough.* If these thoughts and others do rush to your head, how do you respond? Do you just allow them to knock you down and win the fight? *No contest! Uncle! I give up!* Do you realize that thinking these thoughts does not mean that they are true?

Jesus thought some "negative" thoughts while in the desert after his baptism. Satan's suggestions surely came to Jesus through his mind since he was tempted in the same way we are tempted.[5] Because the thoughts did not square with God's word, Jesus recognized them as attacks from the evil one. He did not roll over and play dead. He did not concede or say, "No contest." He did not cower, lick his wounded self-esteem and feel sorry for himself. He did battle against negative, untrue thoughts, and he expects you to do the same.

I know a woman who is very unhappy in her current job, but when I call her to take the risk to pray, trust God and be open to anything else he wants to bring her, she backs off. She falls prey to

[5] Hebrews 2:17-18, 4:15

the negative thoughts that have plagued her much of her life. I have counseled her either to take a faith-risk or to become content where she is. Complaining is not an option.

In order to deal with the negative thoughts, I encourage you to list every one that you can identify on the left side of a page of paper. Then on the right, beside each thought, write what the Holy Spirit through the Bible says back to the thoughts. That's what Jesus did as he did spiritual battle. Every counterattack began with "It is written." If you are stuck on any of them, ask someone else to help you.

If we give in to negative, faith-robbing thoughts, we are being too lazy to fight the good fight and to win the battle with the help of our God.

A Misunderstanding of Putting the Kingdom First

This last buddy of complacency may seem like a strange one with a long name. But, believe me, it belongs in this notorious group! This one takes a lot of discernment to ferret out.

In the church some people have had the mistaken idea that since their mission in life is to be about the business of Jesus (seeking and saving the lost), it doesn't matter what kind of job they have. They reason, *I'll just do some kind of work to get enough money to live on. I won't do anything that challenges me or requires too much of me. Then I can save myself to "crank the ministry" when I get off at 5:00 every day. It would be unspiritual of me to go after a better job because I would, of necessity, have to give less to my ministry.*

Meanwhile, disciples and nondisciples both may look at this

"spiritual" person and say, "She's a loser. I have no respect for her. She has a college degree and does nothing with it. And she wants to give me some kind of guidance for my life? Forget it!"

To be about our ministry is to go into our daily worlds and be a godly example to those with whom we work and interact. We shine out the light of the gospel as we deal with challenging deadlines in a different way than others. We shine like stars in the universe when we manage people with the skills we learned from the manager who was the Son of God. We do not hide our lights under the bushel when we are diligent in our work and are quick to volunteer for the jobs no one else is willing to do. We show people how to live when we have integrity about our work and are not driven by selfish ambition. How can we lead others to walk with Jesus unless we walk the paths they walk and show them how to do it?

Certainly, though, we must sometimes turn down assignments or promotions because they would not be best for our spiritual life or our family life. *Willingness* to take on more responsibility is not the same as *deciding* to take on more responsibility. For example, someone might turn down job opportunities because of any of the following: extensive travel, extended hours, the need to take work home at night, expectation of working on Sundays, etc.

Spiritual discernment is always a must! The issue is not a lack of willingness; it is simply discerning God's will. Work must never be lord! It is not a disgrace to ask for or to accept a "demotion" because your job is keeping you from being your best for God and for others, especially your family. Working mothers, you have to be especially discerning. You are the emotional, nurturing center of your family. Never sacrifice your children at the altar of career advancement. Pray and get much advice in this area. Unless you are at peace with your decisions and their impact on the family, guilt will eat you alive!

A young man named Dave shared his process of determining whether his job was best for the kingdom and for his personal ministry:

> I was in a career in golf-course management for four successful years. At the course where I worked, I met a man named Sean, who invited me to church; and a month later I was baptized.
>
> I had a good year at my job in many ways, but was not happy. I didn't feel I was making enough of an impact. I was in an intensely unspiritual environment. Fortunately, God saw to it that Sean was there, but outside of that, it was a struggle. Also, I felt the expectations were much greater than the compensation. I was working six days a week, nine to ten hours a day, which was expected by my bosses. I looked down the road four or five years and decided that if I wanted to have a family and wanted to keep God first in my life, I would have to make a change. I didn't want to keep missing holidays and gatherings of the disciples because of my job. So I handed in my resignation.
>
> I was totally sold out to the idea that God does have a plan to prosper me (Jeremiah 29:11). The decision was not easy to make. My family wasn't thrilled. My boss tried to talk me out of it, which was challenging because I started to have some doubts about having made the right decision. I got a ton of advice from people in the kingdom, but the decision ultimately came down to this: Am I living according to God's will? I did not believe the career in

golf was God's will for me. Even though the future was sketchy at best, I just knew he would bless me because I was going after him. Basically, through faith, I decided to make my move.

The last few months have not been easy. But through it all, God has been gracious. Today, I am working for an insurance company in the corporate communications unit, which is great because I finally have a job that relates to my degree in communications. I am also working just forty hours a week, but earn a little more than I was earning as a golf course general manager. Additionally, I'm dating steady and leading a family group in the church, both of which occurred since I left my old job.

If there is any advice I can offer someone struggling with a career decision, it would be this: Get lots of advice; make sure the decision is a spiritual one and not based on emotion; go after God's will and don't be afraid to take a risk.

This brother pretty well sums up the type of approach and attitude we need to have in discerning God's will for us in our job situations.

Suggestions for the Job Search

If, through prayer and advice, you are convinced that you need to be looking for another job, here are a few suggestions to help you in your search:

- If you have been fired or laid off or are insecure about your abilities, you need to build confidence that you can be productive and effective. Greg Dillon, a disciple who often counsels people in making career changes, gave this suggestion: Write down a list of fifty accomplishments (defining "accomplishment" as any time in your life that you went after a goal and overcame obstacles to achieve it). He did the exercise himself when making a difficult career change, and found it to be very encouraging. The accomplishments might range from completing a badge in scouting, to receiving certification in a Red Cross life-saving course, to passing a test in high school, to landing an account in advertising. You must keep thinking and listing until you come up with fifty.

- In order to determine the type of job in which you would thrive, consider your talents, skills, training and any threads of interest that might emerge from your "fifty accomplishments" list. Greg suggests that you narrow down the possibilities and talk with people who are currently in any of the jobs that interest you. Ask them questions such as "What is your typical day like?" "What are the good points and bad points of this particular job?" You would be surprised how willing people are to take a few minutes to talk with you about their jobs. (You have not because you ask not.)

- Read a book such as *What Color Is Your Parachute?*[6] The author, Richard Bolles, publishes an updated guide every year in order to stay abreast of the latest available information in the job market. He guides you through certain exercises to help you ascertain your "core competencies" in order to know which type of career is best for you. He also offers helpful input on resumes and interviews.

- Bottom line: You must be willing to go through a process of evaluation and research in order to make an enlightened decision. If you try to switch career tracks too quickly, expect a major derailment…and a big mess to clean up!

[6] Richard Bolles, *What Color Is Your Parachute?* (Berkeley, California: Ten Speed Press, 1997).

- You may find it helpful to consult a career counselor. Find one who is recommended by someone you know and trust. He or she will give you standardized aptitude tests and direction in choosing a new career.

Greg offers several guidelines to keep in mind when going through the interviewing process:

- Interview for practice. That is, accept interviews even if you don't think the job is what you are looking for. You might be pleasantly surprised, and you will also get experience in being interviewed.

- Don't assume that you want the job. Don't be a beggar. Ask questions and be discerning. In fact, interview the interviewer.

- Dress well. Get fashion advice if you need it.

- Find out as much about the company as you can by asking people, searching the Internet, etc. Prospective employers are not impressed with people who have not done their homework.

- Know yourself: your strengths and weaknesses. Present your weaknesses in a positive way.

- Most important: Pray for direction from God. Pray that he will give you and your spiritual advisors wisdom, that he will bring the right people and job information into your life, that he will put you right where he wants you...to his glory.

If you ever meet Francie, please ask her to read this chapter. She should realize that there are certain aspects of working in the secular workplace that will not change no matter where she works or what she does. People are people. Sin is sin. And the world is the world. She should also realize that there is no real security in any job—only in Jesus. If she trusts in him, even if the rug of a job is pulled out from under her, he will never leave her. And lastly, she should probably try to find something in the field that she truly enjoys. She will have a greater possibility of making an impact on others if she experiences more satisfaction in her job. No matter what happens at work, she should have her focus on responding as Jesus would. Her workmates will probably be more open to hearing about a relationship with Jesus when their world is tumbling down around them.

And if you *are* Francie, pray, get advice, trust God and take faith-risks as you determine his will for your life.

A Fresh Cup of Life

Have you ever thought or said, "I hate my job"? If so, what reasons did you list for disliking it so much?

Would you say you tend toward being content or complacent? Ask a friend how she sees you.

If you tend toward complacency, which of the four "buddies" of complacency do you know the best? What will you do to change in this area?

Do you believe that God wants you to change careers or jobs? If yes, why? What will be your first step? If no, how do you see your talents being used effectively in your present career or job?

Do you know "Francie"? That is, do you know someone who is discontent in their job situation? How will you help and encourage her or him?

Are you "Francie"? If yes, will you commit yourself to "pray, get advice, trust God and take faith-risks as you determine his will for your life"?

Through our ups and downs,
God will be filling our cups with his love,
his grace, his forgiveness
and his purpose

FINAL THOUGHTS

༄

With God's Help

The Balancing Act

My goal in this book was to cover topics for working women that would be relevant to singles and marrieds. It is my desire in the future to write another book to specifically address the needs of working marrieds and moms. For that reason I did not speak at length to the issues of balancing work, family and ministry time. But I do feel the need to speak to the general need that we all have to live a balanced life. The elements may differ, but as women and as disciples we have many life-things to balance: Relationship with God. Friendships. Marriage. Job. Parenting. Discipling. Outreach. Roommate relationships.

Who gets the main course of our lives? Who gets the dessert? Who gets the leftovers?

Balance is a tricky thing—hard to keep, easy to lose.

Sometimes we think that the gift of more hours in a day would be a solution. I say nay. More hours would simply give us more time to balance. In the same way, sometimes we think, "If I had a bigger house, I would have more space for things, and therefore, I would be neater." Again, I say nay. More house will simply allow us to have more things. If we are not organized with little space, we will not be organized with more space.

The solution is not being given more time; it is learning to use effectively the time we are given. The balancing act of life is a tough one, to be sure. But we must take it on with the energy and focus afforded us by God's direction and grace.

When the weight of life-things is constantly changing, you must constantly work on keeping them balanced. My daughter may be sick today and therefore, she needs extra attention. Tomorrow I may have a deadline at work, so dinner will have to be more simple than usual. The next day, I may be feeling separated from a friend, so I will use time and energy to call her instead of doing a million other things I could do. I need to make sure my husband and I get some romantic time, so I may decide to fix a nice, candle-lit dinner for Saturday night.

Choices. Choices. Choices. We can decide whether we allow these constant choices to exhaust us, or to invigorate us. Remember that Jesus was willing to confine himself to the limit of twenty-four hours per day also. He kept his focus clear and his priorities straight by keeping his relationship with the Father strong (Mark 1:35-39).

Maintaining balance in our lives is much like driving a car: In order to go straight, you have to continually adjust the steering wheel to the right or to the left. The variables of wheel balance, wind, and road surface call for constant readjustment. To drive is to accept the left-and-right nature of the steering process. How we would love to "set" our lives: this much time and energy in this area, this much in that area, etc., until it is all measured and spread out, never to be apportioned again. But it simply does not work that way. The variables of events, emotions and needs call for constant readjustment. To live is to accept the left-and-right nature of the balancing process.

So, where is God in all this? Right there with us. His promise is sure:

> "Can a mother forget the baby at her breast
>   and have no compassion on the child she has borne?
> Though she may forget,
>   I will not forget you!
> See, I have engraved you on the palms of my hands;
>   your walls are ever before me" (Isaiah 49:15-16).

He is always with us. He will continually help us to make right choices and will continually forgive us if we make wrong ones:

> In all your ways acknowledge him,
>   and he will make your paths straight (Proverbs 3:6).
>
> For he [the Lord] guards the course of the just
>   and protects the way of his faithful ones (Proverbs 2:8).

The key is to seek his will, get lots of advice and trust in his grace. God is working in our lives even when we are not specifically thinking about or doing something in a particular area, because as disciples we have entrusted it all to him.

Our need to maintain balance in our lives simply causes us to draw closer to God and to his Son whom we follow. Jesus is the one in whom all things hold together, the one who keeps the whole universe balanced. Surely he can help us have balance in our lives. We must trust in him daily to help us apportion our time and energy. If we try to do it by relying on ourselves and our own discernment, we will be driven to guilt, confusion, frustration and even bitterness. He knows us; "he knows how we are formed, he remembers that we are dust" (Psalm 103:14). And he loves us and helps us when we are simply seeking to do his will. He will give us all we need to please him:

> His divine power has given us everything we need for life and godliness through our knowledge of him who called us by his own glory and goodness (2 Peter 1:3).

A Fresh Cup of Life

You prepare a table before me
in the presence of my enemies.
You anoint my head with oil;
my cup overflows.
Psalm 23:5

God seats us at his table and stands poised above us with his pitcher full of life. We need only to lift our cups. Jesus came that we might "have life, and have it to the full."[1] And when he fills our cups to overflowing with his life, he makes our "love increase and overflow for each other and for everyone else."[2]

To be sure, life will have its share of challenges and hardships, both on and off the job. Things will not always "go our way." But in it all, through our ups and downs, God will keep filling our cups with his love, his grace, his forgiveness and his purpose.

So keep your cup with you all day long. Let him fill it early in the morning. Let it overflow with "sweet water" during your commute. Visit the spiritual "bubbler" throughout the day. Jesus promises that the water he gives us will become in us "a spring of water welling up to eternal life."[3] Drink deeply. Stay faithful. Share with others who are thirsty.

With God's help you can stay spiritually alive from 9 to 5!

[1] John 10:10
[2] 1 Thessalonians 3:12
[3] John 4:14

Other Books from
Discipleship Publications International

THE DAILY POWER SERIES
Series Editors: Thomas and Sheila Jones

Thirty Days at the Foot of the Cross
A study of the central issue of Christianity

First...the Kingdom
A study of the Sermon on the Mount

The Mission
The inspiring task of the church in every generation

Teach Us to Pray
A study of the most vital of all spiritual disciplines

To Live Is Christ
An interactive study of the Letter to the Philippians

Glory in the Church
God's plan to shine through his church

The Heart of a Champion
Spiritual inspiration from Olympic athletes

Jesus with the People
Encountering the heart and character of Jesus

Hope for a Hurting World
God's love for the poor and needy

MARRIAGE AND FAMILY

The Disciple's Wedding
Planning a Wedding That Gives Glory to God
by Nancy Orr

Friends and Lovers
Marriage As God Designed it
by Sam and Geri Laing

Raising Awesome Kids in Troubled Times
by Sam and Geri Laing

Let It Shine
Teen Quiet-Time Book
edited by Tom and Sheila Jones

Take Hold of Life!
Teen Quiet-Time Journal
edited by Sheila Jones

ESPECIALLY FOR WOMEN

Our Beginning
Genesis Through the Eyes of a Woman
by Kay Summers McKean

The Fine Art of Hospitality
Sharing Your Heart and Your Home with Others
edited by Sheila Jones

The Fine Art of Hospitality Handbook
Tips and Recipes
edited by Sheila Jones and Betty Dyson

She Shall Be Called Woman
Volume 1: Old Testament Women
edited by Sheila Jones and Linda Brumley

She Shall Be Called Woman
Volume 2: New Testament Women
edited by Sheila Jones and Linda Brumley

GROWING IN CHRIST

Discipling
God's Plan to Train and Transform His People
by Gordon Ferguson

The Victory of Surrender
by Gordon Ferguson

TAPED RESOURCES

Out of the Pit
by Dr. Hardy Tillman

More Than Conquerors
by Dr. Hardy Tillman

Discipling
by Gordon Ferguson

Dating in the Kingdom
by Jim and Theresa Brown

Order from DPI
One Merrill street
Woburn, MA 01801
call toll-free
1-888-DPI-BOOK
outside U.S. 617-938-3796
FAX 617-937-3889
http:/www.dpibooks.com